RENEW INTERNATIONAL

WHY CATHOLIC?
JOURNEY THROUGH THE CATECHISM

Pray

RENEW
INTERNATIONAL

The publisher gratefully acknowledges use of the following:

Scripture quotations from the *New Revised Standard Version Bible* (containing the Old and New Testaments with the Apocryphal/Deuterocanonical Books), © 1989 by the Division of Christian Education of the National Council of the Churches of Christ in the U.S.A. are used with permission. All rights reserved.

English translation of the *Catechism of the Catholic Church for the United States of America* © 1994, United States Conference of Catholic Bishops–Libreria Editrice Vaticana. English translation of the *Catechism of the Catholic Church:* Modifications from the *Editio Typica* © 1997, United States Conference of Catholic Bishops–Libreria Editrice Vaticana. Used with permission.

The United States Catholic Catechism for Adults © 2006 United States Conference of Catholic Bishops. Used with permission.

For online access to an interactive site allowing users to search the full text of the *Catechism of the Catholic Church,* go to: www.vatican.va/archive/ENG0015/_INDEX.HTM

Excerpts from *Basil in Blunderland* by Cardinal Basil Hume © 1997 Basil Hume. Darton, Longman and Todd Ltd., pp. 77, 79. Used with permission.

Excerpt from the spiritual journal of Raïssa Maritain, cited in *Blessed among all Women* © 2005 by Robert Ellsberg. The Crossroad Publishing Company, New York, p. 244. See: Raïssa Maritain, *Raïssa's Journal* (Magi Books, Albany, N.Y. 1974)

Quotations from Dorothy Day are from the Dorothy Day Library on the Web at http://www.catholicworker.org/dorothyday.

Poem by Dr. Irma Chávez used with permission.

Quotation of St. Bernardine of Siena is from his sermon *De glorioso Nomine Jesu Christi,* available on the Vatican web site, www.vatican.va

Quotation from Thea Bowman reprinted from Thea Bowman, *In My Own Words,* compilation © 2009 by Maurice J. Nutt . Used with permission of Liguori Publications, www.liguori.org.

Simone Weil quotation on the Lord's Prayer from *Waiting for God* © 1951 by G.P. Putnam's Sons. All rights reserved. Reprinted by HarperPerrenial, a Division of HarperCollins Publishers, pp. 226-227.

All of the quotes from papal and conciliar documents used in this book are from the English translation as presented by the Vatican website, www.vatican.va.

NIHIL OBSTAT
Monsignor James M. Cafone, S.T.D.
Censor Librorum

IMPRIMATUR
Most Reverend John J. Myers, J.C.D., D.D.
Archbishop of Newark

Cover design by James F. Brisson;
Book design and layout by Kathrine Forster Kuo

ISBN 978-1-935532-60-6
(2007 edition ISBN 978-1-935532-02-6)

RENEW International
1232 George Street
Plainfield, NJ 07062-1717
Phone: 908-769-5400
Fax: 908-769-5560
www.renewintl.org
www.WhyCatholic.org

Printed and bound in the United States of America.

Contents

Acknowledgments

RENEW International gratefully acknowledges those who have contributed to this work:

Piloters

Members of small Christian communities who piloted the materials and offered helpful insights.

Music References

All of the songs suggested in this book are available on a CD produced by RENEW International. See more details on page 93; full details at **www.renewintl.org/store**

The publishers of copyright songs suggested in this book are:

Birdwing Music
Care of Brentwood-Benson
Music Publishing
5409 Maryland Way, Ste 200
Brentwood, TN 37027
Phone 615-371-1320
www.brentwood-benson.com

GIA Publications, Inc.
7404 South Mason Avenue
Chicago, IL 60638
Phone 800-442-1358 or 708-496-3800
Fax 708-496-3828
Website www.giamusic.com
E-mail custserv@giamusic.com

Oregon Catholic Press Publications
5536 NE Hassalo
Portland, OR 97213
Phone 800-LITURGY (548-8749)
Fax 800-4-OCP-FAX (462-7329)
Website www.ocp.org
E-mail liturgy@ocp.org

White Dove
White Dove Productions, Inc.
Phone 520-219-3824
Website
www.whitedoveproductions.com
E-mail
info@whitedoveproductions.com

World Library Publications
3708 River Road, Suite 400
Franklin Park, IL 60131
Phone 800-566-6150
Website www.wlpmusic.com

Foreword

My calling as a bishop challenges me to ever seek means to assist solid faith formation and growth in holiness. Foundational in meeting this need is the *Catechism of the Catholic Church*, which so magnificently conveys the wisdom of the Holy Spirit in guiding the Church's tradition in following Jesus Christ.

The Introduction to the U.S. bishops' document *Our Hearts Were Burning Within Us* speaks of how disciples of Jesus share in proclaiming the Good News to the entire world.

Every disciple of the Lord Jesus shares in this mission. To do their part, adult Catholics must be mature in faith and well equipped to share the Gospel, promoting it in every family circle, in every church gathering, in every place of work, and in every public forum. They must be women and men of prayer whose faith is alive and vital, grounded in a deep commitment to the person and message of Jesus.

Why Catholic? Journey through the Catechism is well designed to enable this goal to become reality. It faithfully breaks open the contents of the *Catechism* for reflection and assimilation by individuals or participants in small faith-sharing groups. The sharing enables participants to take greater personal ownership of their faith and to move from an inherited faith to deep faith conviction.

This exploration of divinely revealed truth has a formative effect on peoples' lives. The "yes" of consent to faith emulates Mary's fiat, her "yes" to God's will. A prayerful openness to God's will is the path to holiness.

Why Catholic? seeks to be an instrument for faith formation and a call to holiness. Saints in everyday life are the strength of the Church, which is always renewing itself in fidelity to the mission of Christ and in service to the needs of our society. I heartily commend this effort in making the *Catechism of the Catholic Church* more accessible to the faithful.

Most Reverend John J. Myers, J.C.D., D.D.
Archbishop of Newark

Presenting RENEW International

Why Catholic? Journey through the Catechism is a four-year process of evangelization and adult faith formation developed by RENEW International.

The RENEW process, both parish-based and diocese-wide, was first developed and implemented in the Archdiocese of Newark, New Jersey. Its success there led other dioceses, in the United States, Canada, and in other countries to bring RENEW to their people and parish communities. In the three decades since its vibrant beginnings, RENEW International has touched the lives of 25 million people in over 155 dioceses in the United States, Canada, and 22 other countries throughout the world. RENEW International has grown organically from its original single RENEW process. Materials and training have been offered in over 40 languages—not just translated but adapted to specific cultures. We have added specific pastoral outreach to campuses and to young adults in their 20s and 30s. We have incorporated prison ministry and provided resources for the visually impaired.

The very core of all of these processes remains the same: to help people become better hearers and doers of the Word of God. We do this by encouraging and supporting the formation of small communities who gather prayerfully to reflect on and share the Word of God, to make better connections between faith and life, and to live their faith more concretely in family, work, and community life.

As a not-for-profit organization, our pastoral outreach is sustained in part from the sales of our publications and resources and the stipends we receive for the services provided to parishes and dioceses. However, our priority is always to serve all parishes who desire to renew their faith and build the Church, regardless of their economic situation. We have been able to fulfill this mission not only in the inner city and rural areas in the United States, but also in the developing world, especially Latin America and Africa, thanks to donations and charitable funding.

As you meet in your small group, we invite you to take a few moments to imagine the great invisible network of others, here in North America and on the other continents. They gather, as you do, in small Christian communities, around the Word of God present in the Scripture, striving to hear and act upon that Word. Keep them in your prayer: a prayer of thanksgiving for the many graces we have experienced; a prayer that the Spirit will guide all of us as we explore *Why Catholic? Journey Through the Catechism.*

Introduction

Welcome to *Why Catholic? Journey through the Catechism.*

This four-book series was developed by RENEW International to provide a faith-sharing process for small communities, while unfolding the riches of the *Catechism of the Catholic Church* and the *United States Catholic Catechism for Adults,* both of which are published by the United States Conference of Catholic Bishops. By using these materials, we hope, participants will be encouraged to study both catechisms in even greater depth, allowing the teachings within to illuminate their faith and promote an active response in love.

You are about to journey forward with *PRAY: Christian Prayer.* This book explores how we nurture our relationship with God through prayer.

Why Catholic? is designed to highlight select teachings around which faith sharing may take place, rather than present a compendium or total summary of the catechisms. By nourishing and strengthening women and men in all callings, *Why Catholic?* can serve as an essential tool on the journey to mature Christian faith. We hope that the process will also enable participants to discover and embrace their own personal faith stories and allow them to reflect on, and answer, the questions, "What does it mean to be Catholic? How did I become Catholic? Why do I remain Catholic?"

Why Catholic? is also designed to balance prayer, sharing on Scripture, and reflection on the teachings of our faith, providing a full and fruitful faith-sharing experience for participants. While a prayerful listening to and reflection on Scripture is an integral part of each session, *Why Catholic?* is not meant to be a Scripture study.

Why Catholic? is designed to correspond to the four pillars of the *Catechism of the Catholic Church* and its complement, the *United States Catholic Catechism for Adults.* The three other books in the *Why Catholic?* series are: *BELIEVE: Profession of Faith; CELEBRATE: Sacraments; and LIVE: Christian Morality.* If you are gathering in a small community, you may wish to meet either in two six-week blocks of time or during twelve consecutive weeks to allow one week per session.

In addition, we recommend participants keep a journal and, following each session, spend some time journaling key beliefs of the Catholic faith, along with their personal insights. The journal may serve as a valuable meditation tool as well as a springboard for sharing faith with others.

Throughout the *Why Catholic?* series, direct reference is made to both the *Catechism of the Catholic Church* and the *United States Catholic Catechism for Adults*. This material is identified as (*CCC*) and (*USCCA*) respectively. An excellent explanation of the relationship between the two catechisms can be found at the website of the United States Catholic Conference of Bishops: www.usccbpublishing.org/client/client_pdfs/Q&A_on_USCCA.pdf

We pray that your experience with *Why Catholic?* will lead to a closer, more vibrant relationship with our loving God and your community of faith.

Faith-Sharing Principles and Guidelines

When we gather as Christians to share our faith and grow together in community, it is important that we adhere to certain principles. The following Theological Principles and Small Community Guidelines will keep your community focused and help you to grow in faith, hope, and love.

Principles

- God leads each person on his or her spiritual journey. This happens in the context of the Christian community.

- Christ, the Word made flesh, is the root of Christian faith. It is because of Christ, and in and through him, that we come together to share our faith.

- Faith sharing refers to the shared reflections on the action of God in one's life experience as related to Scripture and the faith of the Church. Faith sharing is not discussion, problem solving, or Scripture study. The purpose is an encounter between a person in the concrete circumstances of his or her life and a loving God, leading to a conversion of heart.

- The entire faith-sharing process is an expression of prayerful reflection.

Guidelines

- Constant attention to respect, honesty, and openness for each person will assist the community's growth.

- Each person shares on the level where he or she feels comfortable.

- Silence is a vital part of the total process. Participants are given time to reflect before any sharing begins, and a period of comfortable silence might occur between individual sharings.

- Persons are encouraged to wait to share a second time until others who wish to do so have contributed.

- The entire community is responsible for participating and faith sharing.

- Confidentiality is essential, allowing each person to share honestly.
- Action flowing out of the small-community meetings is essential for the growth of individuals and the community.

A Note to Small Community Leaders

Small Community Leaders are …

- People who encourage participation and the sharing of our Christian faith.
- People who encourage the spiritual growth of the community and of its individual members through communal prayer, a prayerful atmosphere at meetings, and daily prayer and reflection on the Scriptures.
- People who move the community to action to be carried out between meetings. They are not satisfied with a self-centered comfort level in the community but are always urging that the faith of the community be brought to impact on participants' daily lives and the world around them.
- Community builders who create a climate of hospitality and trust among all participants.

Small Community Leaders are not …

- Theologians: The nature of the meeting is faith sharing. Should a theological or scriptural question arise, the leader should turn to the pastor or staff to seek guidance.
- Counselors: The small communities are not intended for problem solving. This is an inappropriate setting to deal with emotionally laden issues of a personal nature. The leader is clearly not to enter the realm of treating people with emotional, in-depth feelings such as depression, anxiety, or intense anger. When someone moves in this direction, beyond faith sharing, the leader should bring the community back to faith sharing. With the help of the pastor or staff, the person should be advised to seek the assistance of professional counseling.
- Teachers: The leaders are not teachers. Their role is to guide the process of the faith sharing as outlined in the materials.

N.B. *SOWING SEEDS: Essentials for Small Community Leaders* provides a comprehensive collection of pastoral insights and practical suggestions to assist small community leaders in their crucial role of facilitating a *Why Catholic?* small community. Available from RENEW International's secure online webstore: www.renewintl.org/store. See page 94.

How to Use This Book

Whenever two or more of us gather in the name of Jesus, we are promised that Christ is in our midst (see Matthew 18:20). This book helps communities to reflect on the Scriptures, the *Catechism of the Catholic Church* and the *United States Catholic Catechism for Adults*. It is most helpful if some members of the group or the group as a whole have the Scriptures and one, or both, of the catechisms at their meeting.

Those who have met in small communities will be familiar with the process. In this book based on the *Catechism*, however, there is particular emphasis on the great mysteries of our faith. These reflections make demands upon our reflective nature and help in the formation of our Catholic values. **Therefore, it is important that participants carefully prepare for the session before coming to the meeting.** They are encouraged to read and reflect on the session itself, the Scripture passage(s) cited, and the sections or pages of the *CCC* and the *USCCA* referenced.

If the community has not met before or if participants do not know each other, take time for introductions and to get acquainted. People share most easily when they feel comfortable and accepted in a community.

Prayer must always be at the heart of our Christian gatherings. Following any necessary introductions, sessions begin with a time of prayer—Lifting Our Hearts. There are suggested songs, but other appropriate songs may be used. All of the suggested songs are available on the CD *Pray: Songs for Faith Sharing,* produced by RENEW International. Most of these songs can be found in the standard parish worship collections. If songs are copyrighted, remember you need to request permission before making copies of either the words or the music. The contact information for permissions can be found on page iv.

Each week, an action response— Living the Good News—is recommended. After the first week, the leader encourages participants to share how they put their faith in action by following through on their Living the Good News commitment from the previous session.

Following Lifting Our Hearts, and Living the Good News, there is an initial reflection on the *Catechism* entitled Reflection 1. The next section, Pondering the Word, offers a Scripture reference that one participant proclaims aloud from the Bible. Together, the *Catechism* and Scripture selections will give the community members the opportunity to reflect on what Jesus has said and to share their faith on the particular topic. Sharing could take about 15 minutes.

Next, the small community continues Reflection 2 and then

considers the Sharing Our Faith questions.

Faith-sharing groups vary greatly in their background and composition. In some sessions, the group may wish to start with the question: What insights into my faith did I gain from this session? Explain. Allow approximately 25 minutes for Sharing Our Faith, making sure the last question is always considered.

In coming to closure, each session offers some ideas for an individual or group action—Living the Good News. Here, participants reflect on how God is inviting them to act during the coming week—how to bring their faith into their daily lives. The ideas presented are merely suggestions. It is important that group members choose an action that is both measurable and realistic.

Each session then concludes with Lifting Our Hearts.

How we can pray right from our hearts

As we gather with others, we are sometimes invited to offer spontaneous prayers. You will be invited to do so several times during these sessions. There is a widely used practice that can make it easier to compose a prayer on the spot; it begins with remembering the words *you, who, do,* and *through.* These words represent familiar elements in prayer.

You: We begin our prayers by addressing and praising God with one of several traditional titles such as "Almighty God," "Ever-loving God," "Heavenly Father," or "Dear Lord."

Who: We acknowledge what God has done for the world and for us. This could include such statements as "who created us to love and serve you," "who give us grace in your sacraments," "who gave your only Son to save us from sin and death," "who made the world with all of its wonders," or "who gathered us here to serve your people."

Do: We ask God to do something for us, for others, or for the world at large: "help us to teach our students with wisdom and gentleness," "help those who do not enjoy economic or political freedom," "help us to respond to the needs of the poor," or "quiet our minds and hearts as we experience this retreat."

Through: We pray through Jesus and with the Holy Spirit.

And so, for example, a person who is invited to offer an opening prayer at a meeting of Catholic school parents might say, "Almighty God, who gave us your only Son as our first and best teacher, help us in what we say and what we do to faithfully pass on his teaching to our children. We ask this through Jesus Christ, our Lord, who lives and reigns with you and the Holy Spirit now and forever. Amen."

Liturgical colors can add to prayerful atmosphere

When we gather for faith sharing, it is important to be in a prayerful and reflective environment. At the beginning of each session of this process, there are suggestions for displaying on a small table the Bible, a candle, and other symbolic items that might contribute to a suitable atmosphere.

In each session, one suggestion is to decorate the table with the color of the liturgical season. The liturgical colors are white, violet, green, red, black, and rose. The *Roman Missal* prescribes the color to be used in the three liturgical seasons and on specific days, such as Passion Sunday and Pentecost, when the liturgical color is red. In general, however, the colors are white for the Easter and Christmas seasons and on holy days including the Assumption (August 15), the Ascension (forty days after Easter),

All Saints (November 1), and the Immaculate Conception (December 8); violet during Lent and Advent; and green during Ordinary Time.

Sharing beyond the Small Community

As a community, you will be using this book as the focus for your sharing. You should consider how the fruits of your sharing can be taken beyond the confines of this group. For example, if you are parents, you could be asking what part of your faith exploration can be shared with your children. RENEW International has designed a resource, entitled RENEWING FAMILY FAITH, to help you achieve exactly this.

RENEWING FAMILY FAITH offers a two-page full-color bulletin for every session contained in the *Why Catholic?* faith-sharing books. You will find a full description of this invaluable resource on page 93.

Suggested Format of the Sharing Sessions (1½ hours)

Introductions (when the group is new or when someone joins the group)

Lifting Our Hearts	10 minutes
Sharing the Good News	5 minutes
Reflection 1	10 minutes
Scripture: Pondering the Word and Sharing Question	15 minutes
Reflection 2	10 minutes
Sharing Our Faith	25 minutes
Living the Good News	10 minutes
Lifting Our Hearts	5 minutes

What is Prayer?

Suggested Environment

At the beginning of the opening prayer, burn incense: its rising smoke is a traditional symbol of prayer. As the incense is lit, recite the Scripture verse: "Let my prayer be counted as incense before you" (Psalm 141:2). As an alternative, have a bowl of water on a small table with the scriptural verse, "Oh, everyone who thirsts, come to the waters" (Isaiah 55:1). You may also have a Bible—open to the reading for this session—displayed on a small table along with a burning candle. Consider decorating the table with the color of the liturgical season and other symbols of faith.

In addition, it is helpful to have available the Catechism of the Catholic Church (CCC) *and the* United States Catholic Catechism for Adults (USCCA).

Lifting Our Hearts

Song Suggestion

"Open My Eyes," Jesse Manibusan

Prayer

Prayed together by alternating groups or by participants on alternating sides of the room:

Group 1 Ever-present God,
      we come now to rest in you.
      Our days and weeks are filled
      with activity.

Group 2 But now we want, we need,
      to take this time to calm ourselves,
      to reestablish our priorities,
      and to spend time with you,
      our Creator and friend.

Group 1	Help us to be at peace, to sit in your presence, to ponder how much you love us and are waiting for us to come to you.
Group 2	Increase our faith and hope in your Son, Jesus Christ. We know he is present with us. We thank you for his presence and his everlasting love.
All	**Holy Spirit of love, give us a great desire to pray, to develop that intimacy that you desire with us. Keep us always in your love and grace. We ask this in the name of Jesus Christ and in the power of the Holy Spirit. Amen.**

Reflection 1

Prayer is God's gift

While Cardinal Basil Hume was archbishop of Westminster, England (1976-1999), he vacationed in a big house in Scotland with a family he knew well. The children in the family, Kate and Barney, drew the cardinal into a game of hide-and-seek. He agreed, but immediately wondered when he would observe the half hour of mental prayer that was required of him as a Benedictine monk. But as the game progressed in the nooks and crannies of the house, Cardinal Hume found that he could be alone a few minutes here and there. In those moments, various mundane objects—a clock, a telephone, a staircase, a piano, a medicine cabinet—prompted his thoughts about the spiritual life. In the end, he fulfilled his daily prayer and reached this conclusion:

"Now many of us play hide-and-seek often. We don't play with Kate or Barney, or with any other children. We play with God. It is not that He hides from us, we hide from Him. He is the one who is looking for us, trying to find us. We hide, because we may not be able to face being found…. And yet He goes on searching us out. Why? Because he seeks intimacy with us."

Source: *Basil in Blunderland*, Cardinal Basil Hume, p. 77.

Sharing Question

• In what ways have you experienced God searching for you?

One of the most important questions in the gospels, and one of the most important answers, occur in the account of the death and resurrection of Lazarus (*Jn* 11,1-45). "I am the resurrection and the life," Jesus tells Martha, a sister of Lazarus. "Those who believe in me, even though they die, will live, and everyone who lives and believes in me will never die. Do you believe this?" That's the important question: *"Do you believe this?"* Martha answers, "Yes, Lord, I believe that you are the Christ, the son of God, the one coming into the world." That's the important answer: *"Yes, Lord, I believe … ."* Jesus is asking Martha to accept on faith his identity and his promise. His identity and his promise are part of the great mystery of faith that we Catholic Christians are called, first, to believe. Once we say "I believe" to the mystery of faith, we are called to celebrate it—as we do in liturgy—and to "live from it in a vital and personal relationship with the living and true God. This relationship is prayer" (*CCC*, 2558).

We take part in this relationship best as a natural part of our daily lives, not as a chore that we must attend to. Scripture reminds us, too, that the relationship we form with God in prayer originates with his desire for friendship with us, not with our needs and desires. In the gospel story about the encounter between Jesus and the Samaritan woman, it is Jesus who speaks first, asking the woman for a drink. When the woman expresses her surprise at this breach of cultural norms, Jesus answers: "If you knew the gift of God, and who it is that is saying to you, 'Give me a drink,' you would have asked him, and he would have given you living water" (*Jn* 4:7-10). So, as

God runs to embrace his returning children

"The story of the Prodigal Son teaches us another important point. God seeks us but does not force us. We remain free to be found or not, to return to Him or not. The father in the parable is waiting for his son to return. One day he sees him coming home. 'While he was yet at a distance (v.20),' the father, we are told, 'had compassion and ran and embraced him and kissed him.'That verse 20 has taught me, more than any other passage in the Bible, what God is like. Read it again and again, let your mind dwell on it. Your heart will then begin to warm. When that happens you have been found, and you will not have any desire to hide again."

Cardinal Basil Hume, *Basil in Blunderland*, p. 79.

Cardinal Hume pointed out, it is God, through Jesus, who first seeks us, not the other way around.

We enter this relationship most fruitfully when we recognize that the very invitation to pray is a gift freely given to us by God. We do not pray in order to exalt ourselves. We are not proud or demanding in making our petitions to God; on the contrary, we pray in humility and contrition, acknowledging who God is and who we are (*CCC,* 2559).

Sharing Question

- During what activities of everyday life have you been moved to pray?

Pondering the Word

"Two men went up to the temple to pray"

Luke 18:9-14

Sharing Questions

- Take a moment to reflect on what word, phrase, or image from the scripture passage touches your heart or speaks to your life. Reflect in silence on your thoughts, or share them aloud.
- How do you approach God in prayer?
- What makes you feel humble, fearful, or confident in your relationship with God?

Reflection 2

Being with God

Going "up to the temple" is only one of the many ways, and the "temple" itself—the church—is only one of the many places in which we pray. Prayer is a loving relationship with God, and persons in a loving relationship are present to each other and attentive to each other with little regard for time and place—in other words, whether we pray in church, at home, on the beach, in the forest, or on the bus or train commuting to work. Relationships can suffer from distraction that leads to neglect, and our busy lives provide plenty of distractions. We have jobs to do; children to raise; shopping, cleaning, and gardening to accomplish; exercises to perform; friends to visit, and television series to follow. All of these things are important in their own ways, but together they can consume us. We know, however, that no love relationship grows unless we spend time with those we love. That's what we do in prayer: We spend time with God, putting other things aside, listening and speaking, offering our hearts to the one we love (*CCC*, 2565).

Prayer takes many forms—words, gestures, even silence. "For me," St. Thérèse of Lisieux wrote, "prayer is a surge of the heart; it is a simple look turned toward heaven; it is a cry of recognition and of love, embracing both trial and joy." The *Catechism* reminds us that, regardless of the form, it is the whole person that prays. With respect to the *source* of prayer, however, while Scripture sometimes names the soul or the spirit, it speaks more than a thousand times of the *heart* (*CCC*, 2562). This is not the anatomical heart but "the dwelling-place where I am, where I live … . The heart is our hidden center, beyond the grasp of our reason and of others; only the Spirit of God can fathom the human heart and know it fully. The heart is the place of decision, deeper than our psychic drives. It is the place of truth, where we choose life or death. It is the place of encounter … ." (*CCC*, 2563). The heart is where each of us meets and enters into covenant with God, "covenant" meaning that we align our will to God's will in response to his loving call (*CCC*, 2563, 2564).

For Christians, prayer is a covenant relationship with the Holy Trinity (*CCC*, 2564). The God who lives in communion—three Persons, one Divine Nature—invites us to enter into communion with him, to become one with him, in prayer. "This communion of life is always possible because, through Baptism, we have already been united with

Keeping a journal can enrich prayer

Christians at prayer often find it helpful to engage more fully with their reading and their thoughts by keeping a personal journal. Prayer involves both listening to and responding to God's Word; response can take many forms, including fragments of Scripture or other spiritual reading that you want to recall as well as your notes, poetry, or sketches. What is most important is feeling free to use whatever form allows you to best express what is happening in your heart—anguish, joy, thanksgiving. We don't keep a journal to tell God what he already knows but to learn more and more about ourselves and our relationship with him. A prayer journal can be simply a blank notebook that is compact enough to easily carry with you but expansive enough to let you express yourself. It can also be a book specifically designed for this purpose, such as *GLEANINGS: A Personal Prayer Journal*, available from RENEW International. (See page 94.)

Christ (Cf. *Rom* 6:5). Prayer is *Christian* insofar as it is communion with Christ and extends throughout the Church, which is his Body. Its dimensions are those of Christ's love (Cf. *Eph* 3:18-21)" (CCC, 2565). Thus, in prayer the Holy Spirit moves us toward union with the Persons of the Trinity as well as with one another.

There may be times when we feel that we have lost contact with God or that we are the ones searching for God, but the truth is that God never leaves us. We may even turn from God at times, but he continues to call each of us to turn back and meet him in prayer (CCC, 2567). In prayer, God always makes the first move with his offer of love; our first step in prayer is always a response to God's call. We need only open ourselves to God's love and his tender care. A good way to keep our minds open to his voice is to read books on spirituality and prayer. Such books can keep us focused on our relationship with God while so many important and trivial concerns are competing for our attention.

Sharing Questions

- What place does prayer occupy among the priorities of your daily life?
- Talk about the time you felt closest to God.

Living the Good News

Jesus emphasized the connection between faith and action, between what we believe and what we do. In that spirit, decide on an individual or group action that flows from what you have shared in this session. If you decide to act on your own, share your decision with the group. If you decide on a group action, determine among you which individual members will take responsibility for various aspects of the action.

You are likely to benefit most from taking an action that arises from your own response to the session. However, you can consider one of the following suggestions or use these ideas to help develop one of your own:

- Set up a special room or corner in your home that you designate as a prayer room or prayer corner. Choose a time to pray there together with your family.
- Spend at least fifteen minutes a day in prayer if you do not already do so.
- Keep a prayer journal.

• Research books on prayer and spirituality. Seek suggestions at a retreat house or monastery in your area; ask for recommendations from a knowledgeable person. If your parish does not have a library of books to help people with prayer, inquire about forming a committee to start one.

As my response to the Gospel of Jesus, this week I commit to:

_____

_____

Lifting Our Hearts

Pray together by alternating groups or by participants on alternating sides of the room:

Group 1	Gracious God, you have invited us into a relationship that continues to be fed through the gift of prayer.
Group 2	Our response to you is but a shadow of your unconditional love for us. Your call to relationship is not just at certain times and places but in the daily chores, jobs, distractions, joys, and sorrows of everyday life.
Group 1	Within these times, you desire to comfort, support, encourage, celebrate, and laugh with us. Remind us that our union with you in prayer is but a thought away.
Group 2	We have gathered together in your name with a desire to be more faithful to your call to relationship. Give us ears to always hear your voice, a heart to listen to the message, and a will to live it out.
Group 1	Let the fruits of our prayer touch a world that seeks your peace. You challenge us to be your image and call us to do your work of love in this world.

All   **Let us "go now to love and**
serve the Lord in one another."
We ask this of you who live and reign
as our God, forever and ever. Amen.

Looking Ahead

- Prepare for your next session by prayerfully reading and studying:
  - Session 2: Prayer in the Old Testament;
  - Scripture: Genesis 12:1-9 (The call of Abram); Genesis 15:1-6 (the covenant with Abram).
  - You may also like to read the *United States Catholic Catechism for Adults,* Chapter 35 "God Calls Us to Pray," pages 464-466 on "Old Testament People at Prayer."
  - You may like to consult paragraphs 2568-2597 on prayer in the Old Testament from the *Catechism of the Catholic Church.*
  - Consider reading *Opening to God* by Thomas H. Green, SJ (Ave Maria Press), a guide to prayer that has been helpful to many people at various stages of maturity in their spiritual lives.
- Remember to use RENEWING FAMILY FAITH and its helpful suggestions on how to extend the fruits of your sharing beyond your group, especially to your families. See page 93.

Prayer in the Old Testament

Suggested Environment

You may have a Bible—open to the beginning of the Book of Psalms—displayed on a small table along with a burning candle and a picture or icon of an Old Testament figure, such as Noah, Abraham, Sarah, Moses, Miriam, David, or Esther. Consider decorating the table with the color of the liturgical season and other symbols of faith.

In addition, it is helpful to have available the Catechism of the Catholic Church (CCC) *and the* United States Catholic Catechism for Adults (USCCA).

Begin with a quiet, reflective atmosphere.

Lifting Our Hearts

Song Suggestion

"The Summons" ("Will You Come and Follow Me?"), John Bell

Prayer

Pray together.

Ever-present God,
as we gather to reflect on our faith
we take courage in remembering
that we do not do this alone.

We recall the men and women
who from ancient times
have heard and answered your call
to be united with you in prayer.

We remember Abraham and Sarah,
Moses, Aaron, and Miriam,

Hannah, Esther, and Solomon:
our ancestors in faith.

We hope to gain from their stories
a greater confidence in your mercy,
a firmer commitment to do your will,
and a deeper union with you
and all who love you. Amen.

Sharing Our Good News

*Before continuing, take a few moments to share with the group something
of your experience of prayer since our last meeting, including anything that
might have resulted from "Living the Good News."*

Reflection 1

Walking with God

Dorothy Day's journey to God was indirect, to say the least. In
retrospect, it seems clear that God was calling her from her early
childhood until her baptism at the age of 30. At times she was
enthralled and adopted a life of Scripture reading and prayer; at times
she withdrew and even rejected any notion of piety. Meanwhile, she
became deeply conscious of the needs of exploited workers and of
the poor. She dropped out of college and moved to New York, where
she worked for socialist periodicals and took part in demonstrations
against war and in favor of women's political rights. One of her
relationships led to an abortion that she always regretted, and another
led to the birth, in 1926, of her daughter, Tamar. This was a life-altering
event for Day. After a heartbreaking struggle that ended when she
separated from Tamar's irreligious father, Dorothy Day, feeling the
need to worship God in community, embraced Catholicism and
began writing for Catholic publications. In the 1930s, Day and Peter
Maurin co-founded the Catholic Worker Movement, establishing a
newspaper and a network of houses of hospitality for the poor. For the
balance of her life she was one of the most influential campaigners for
peace, social justice, and economic equality. Throughout the unsettled
life leading up to her baptism and full realization of her vocation,
there were signs of God's call: a Bible she found in the attic, a pious
Methodist neighbor, a Catholic girlfriend who told her stories of the
saints, an Episcopal minister who invited Day and her siblings to
church, her own reading of Thomas á Kempis, St. Augustine, and St.

Teresa of Ávila—and the poor, in whose faces, she said, she saw the face of God.

Sharing Question

• Recall an occasion when you recognized God's call to you in what seemed at the time like a chance meeting or experience.

All religions are evidence of people searching for God. At the same time, as we have seen, God does not wait for us to find him but calls us to meet him in prayer (*CCC*, 2567). God calls, and we respond. It is a drama that has unfolded through the whole history of salvation, just as it unfolded in the life of Dorothy Day.

> "And then I remember we were in the attic. I was sitting behind a table, pretending I was the teacher, reading aloud from a Bible that I had found. Slowly, as I read, a new personality impressed itself on me. I was being introduced to someone and I knew almost immediately that I was discovering God.
>
> "I know that I had just really discovered Him because it excited me tremendously. It was as though life were fuller, richer, more exciting in every way."
>
> —*Dorothy Day*

In the Old Testament, where the origins of that history are recorded, we read how God's loving relationship with us evolved through the experiences of various men and women. In the Book of Genesis, we are told that Abel—a son of Adam and Eve—offered the firstborn of his flock to God; that people at the time of Enosh— grandson of Adam and Eve—"began to invoke the name of the Lord" (*Gn* 4:26); and that the patriarch Enoch "walked with God" (*Gn* 5:22). Also in Genesis we read that Noah—after the flood—made an offering that was pleasing to God and that God blessed Noah (*CCC*, 2569). And so, our early predecessors in faith were aware of, and acknowledged, God's imminent presence in the world and in their lives, as do many people in all religions in our own time.

It is, however, in the account of God's call to Abraham (first known as Abram) that the Old Testament begins to reveal the dimensions of prayer and the place of prayer in salvation history. About 1900 years before the birth of Jesus, God instructed Abraham to migrate to Canaan, promising to give that land to Abraham and his descendants. Abraham obeyed God. In the story of Abraham we see that a heart that embraces God's will is indispensible to a prayerful relationship with God; the value of the words of our prayer depends on that—on embracing the will of God (*CCC*, 2570). Indeed, as Abraham made his way to his destination, he prayed not by speaking but by building two altars to the Lord. Only later do we read Abraham's first spoken prayer, and there we find him asking how it was possible that he would be the father of a nation when he and his wife, Sarah, had no children (*Gn* 15:2-4). "Thus one aspect of the drama of prayer appears from the beginning: the test of faith in the fidelity of God" (*CCC*, 2570).

In the first book of Samuel, we read about Hannah, who was deeply troubled because she had no children. She prayed silently at the temple and confided in the priest Eli, who gave her confidence that God would grant her request. Hannah ultimately had five children, and she dedicated the first one, Samuel, to serve God in the temple. Her beautiful prayer of thanksgiving after the birth of Samuel—"My heart exults in the Lord; my strength is exalted in my God"—echoes in Mary's prayer, the Magnificat, before the birth of Jesus (1 *Sm* 1:1–2:10).

Sharing Question

- Recall an incident or circumstance in your life that has caused you to struggle with your faith in God.

Pondering the Word

Abram did as the Lord had told him

Genesis 15:1-6

Sharing Questions

- Take a moment to reflect on what word, phrase, or image from the scripture passage touches your heart or speaks to your life. Reflect in silence on your thoughts, or share them aloud.

- What God promised must have seemed impossible to Abraham and Sarah. Abraham wondered aloud about that but ultimately accepted God's promises in faith. How does your prayer life with God reflect your faith in his promise of something that seems impossible to many—eternal life?

Reflection 2

Our ancestors in faith teach us to pray

We learn in the Old Testament that a prayer relationship with God involves interaction. Abraham, for example, having learned that

God intended to punish Sodom and Gomorrah for their immorality, questioned God until God agreed to spare the cities if even 10 righteous people remained there (*Gn* 18:20-33). We also read that, before a confrontation with his brother Esau, Abraham's grandson Jacob wrestled all night with a mysterious man who then blessed Jacob and renewed God's promise to Abraham (*Gn* 32:22-30). These accounts of human beings in dynamic relationships with God have given rise to "the symbol of prayer as a battle of faith and as the triumph of perseverance (Cf. *Gn* 32:24-30; *Lk* 18:1-8)" (*CCC*, 2573).

Later, the initiative again came from God as he called upon Moses to demand that the pharaoh of Egypt free the Hebrew people from slavery. Moses agreed only after a long and difficult debate. "But in the dialogue … Moses also learns how to pray: he balks, makes excuses, above all questions …" (*CCC*, 2575). Moses doubted that he could do God's will; God said he could—if he trusted in God's help. Miriam—a prophet and the sister of Moses and Aaron—led the Hebrew women in a song of praise after God had destroyed the

Queen Esther's prayer saves her people

The Book of Esther in the Old Testament provides an example of the importance of depending on God in prayer. Esther, a Jewish orphan who was raised by her cousin Mordecai, became queen of Persia when the king chose her from among women brought to his harem from around the empire. Esther, who on Mordecai's instructions kept her background secret, was troubled about her relationship with a pagan king and she was embarrassed by the crown and other trappings she had to wear in public. Meanwhile, because Mordecai refused to bow to Haman, a high official of the pagan government, Haman convinced the king to order the massacre of all Jews in the empire. Mordecai, reminding Esther of her humble background, urged her to plead with the king to spare the Jewish people. Esther answered that she would be risking her life by entering the king's presence without being summoned, and by revealing that she was a Jew, but Mordecai said that she would die with the rest of her people. Finally, Esther fasted for three days and nights and dressed in mourning with dirt and ashes on her head instead of the precious ointments she was used to. After fasting, she asked for God's help, praying, "My Lord, our King, you alone are God. Help me, who am alone and have no help but you." (*Est* C:14). She approached the king: "I ask that my life be spared, and I beg that you spare the lives of my people" (*Est* 7:3). The king sympathized with Esther, repealed the order, and had the official hanged. Esther's faith and courage and God's saving response are commemorated each year on the feast of Purim.

Egyptian army in the Red Sea: "Sing to the Lord, for he has triumphed gloriously; horse and rider he has thrown into the sea" (*Ex* 15:20-21).

As the conversation continued after the flight from Egypt, God spoke to Moses, as it were, face to face, as a person speaks to a friend. In this relationship, the prayer of Moses on behalf of his people was contemplative: listening repeatedly to God's word, Moses remained faithful to his mission and reassured the Hebrews of God's presence and promise (*CCC*, 2576, 2577). It is in this encounter, too, that Moses provided a striking example of intercessory prayer—not for himself but for his people—a form of prayer that would be expressed most fully in Jesus Christ, the one go-between who takes our intercessions directly to God and brings God's grace to us (*CCC*, 2575).

Prayer continued to flourish among the People of God under the guidance of their leaders (*CCC*, 2578). Among the most prominent of these was King David, traditionally thought to be the source of more than 70 psalms now included in the Bible. "His submission to the will of God, his praise, and his repentance, will be a model for the prayer of the people" (*CCC*, 2579). This prayer consistently expresses a "joyful trust in God" (*CCC*, 2579).

After David died and his son, Solomon, became king, God offered to grant Solomon any request. Solomon prayed for "an understanding mind" so that he could govern Israel. God replied that because Solomon had not prayed for a long life, for wealth, or for the death of his enemies, he would be rewarded with wisdom (1 *Kgs* 3:5-14). Solomon later built the Temple of Jerusalem which was to be the principal place where the people grew in prayer, but the people often became more absorbed in observing rituals than in taking to heart the law of God and practicing it in their lives. Addressing this was the job of the prophets who, like Moses, had "one-on-one" encounters with God and delivered his message to the people and their leaders (*CCC*, 2580, 2581). They didn't shy away from the difficulty of this

Spotlight on the *Catechism*

"These incomparable prayers … embraced every age of history, while being rooted in each moment of time. They were sung at the Temple, in local synagogues, in family settings, on pilgrimages, and in the solitude of personal prayer. They formed the basis of the prayer of Jesus and, as such, can be used to draw us into his prayer as well. The Psalms are part of every celebration of Mass. They also form the heart and soul of the *Liturgy of the Hours*, that public daily prayer of the Church which prolongs the Eucharistic celebration and gives praise to God."

United States Catholic Catechism for Adults, pp. 465-466

mission. "Their prayer is not flight from this unfaithful world, but rather attentiveness to The Word of God. At times their prayer is an argument or a complaint, but it is always an intercession that awaits and prepares for the intervention of the Savior God" (Cf. *Am* 7:2,5; *Isa* 6:5, 8,11; *Jer* 1:6; 15:15-18; 20:7-18) (*CCC*, 2584).

We see that pattern again in the biblical story of Judith, a well-to-do widow who chastised the king and other leaders of Israel for threatening to surrender the kingdom to the surrounding Assyrian army. Judith prayed passionately for God's help and then used subterfuge to enter the Assyrian camp and kill the commander. After the Israelites' successful counterattack, Judith led Israel in a soaring hymn of thanksgiving (*Jdt* 8:1-16:17).

A unique part of the Old Testament is the Book of Psalms, a collection of 150 hymns and prayers that express the personal experiences of the writers or the works of God among his people. Many are laments, others are songs of praise and thanksgiving, some even include curses. Often these modes overlap. Although the vivid and sometimes graphic imagery of the psalms was originally inspired by specific historical events, these are also prayers for the ages. We can read them and meditate on them to let them speak to our own awe at the works of God, our own thanksgiving for what he has done in our lives, our own hopes and needs, our own fears and frustrations and even anger. The psalms were composed in a culture very different from our own, but we can benefit from reading them within the context of our Christian faith. The psalms reflect on the past, and they look ahead to the coming of the Messiah and beyond.

Our own experiences are similar to those of our Hebrew ancestors in faith. God calls us, too, to an intimacy based on love and fidelity. We, too, struggle to know God, not merely to know *about* God. We join the psalmist often in lamenting our sorrows and praising God, sometimes feeling God's love and other times feeling abandoned, sometimes feeling comfort and other times feeling confusion and fear. Through it all, we recognize we are one family with a history of a powerful relationship with God who always reaches out to draw us into a deeper love.

Sharing Questions

- To what extent have you experienced prayer as a conversation or dialogue with God rather than a process in which you speak and God listens?

• How do you think your prayer will be affected by the reflections and sharing in this session?

Living the Good News

Jesus emphasized the connection between faith and action, between what we believe and what we do. In that spirit, decide on an individual or group action that flows from what you have shared in this session. If you decide to act on your own, share your decision with the group. If you decide on a group action, determine among you which individual members will take responsibility for various aspects of the action.

You are likely to benefit most from taking an action that arises from your own response to the session. However, you can consider one of the following suggestions or use these ideas to help develop one of your own:

• Read one Psalm daily, reflecting on the words of praise, thanksgiving, supplication, or trust.

• Pray Psalm 139, a Psalm of David, daily.

• Select one book of the Old Testament to read this week—for example, Hosea, Esther, or Ruth—or read about the experiences of Sarah in the book of Genesis, chapters 12-23.

• Speak with a person of another faith tradition to learn more about his or her prayer traditions.

As my response to the Gospel of Jesus, I commit to:

_____

_____

Lifting Our Hearts

Now let's listen prayerfully again to the hymn. As you listen and for a few moments after the hymn ends, try to reflect on how these words apply to your life: "Will you come and follow me if I but call your name.... Will you use the faith you've found to reshape the world around?"

"The Summons" ("Will You Come and Follow me?") , John Bell

After the hymn and a few moments of silence, pray Psalm 8 together:

O LORD, our Sovereign,
   how majestic is your name in all the earth!

You have set your glory above the heavens.
   Out of the mouths of babes and infants
you have founded a bulwark because of your foes,
   to silence the enemy and the avenger.

When I look at your heavens, the work of your fingers,
   the moon and the stars that you have established;
what are human beings that you are mindful of them,
   mortals that you care for them?

Yet you have made them a little lower than God,
   and crowned them with glory and honor.
You have given them dominion over the works of your hands;
   you have put all things under their feet,
all sheep and oxen,
   and also the beasts of the field,
the birds of the air, and the fish of the sea,
   whatever passes along the paths of the seas.

O LORD, our Sovereign,
   how majestic is your name in all the earth!

Looking Ahead

- Prepare for your next session by prayerfully reading and studying:

  - Session 3: How to Pray;

  - Scripture: 1 Mark 1:32-37 (Jesus prays alone in "a deserted place").

  - You might like to consult the relevant paragraphs in the *Catechism of the Catholic Church:* paragraphs 2598-2622 which present how Jesus prayed (2599-2606), how Jesus teaches us to pray (2607-2615), that Jesus hears our prayers (2616), and the prayer of the Virgin Mary (2617-2619);

  - You might want to read the *United States Catholic Catechism for Adults*, Chapter 35 "God Calls Us to Pray," pp. 470-472 on "Prayer in Communion with Mary."

- Remember to use RENEWING FAMILY FAITH and its helpful suggestions on how to extend the fruits of your sharing beyond your group, especially to your families. See page 93.

How to Pray

You may have a Bible—open to the reading for this session—displayed on a small table along with a statue of Mary and a burning candle. Consider decorating the table with the color of the liturgical season and other symbols of faith.

In addition, it is helpful to have available the Catechism of the Catholic Church (CCC) *and the* United States Catholic Catechism for Adults (USCCA).

Begin with a quiet, reflective atmosphere.

Lifting Our Hearts

Song Suggestion

"Holy is His Name," John Michael Talbot

Prayer

Pray together.

Jesus, teach us how to pray.
> As we gather here, and in our daily lives,
> let us feel the need for prayer,
> and an ardent desire to encounter you.

Remake us, open us, strengthen us,
> and increase within us faith, hope, and love.

Mary, our mother, given to us by your Son,
> teach us to pray as you taught him.

Pray for us, too, O Mary, our mother,
> that we will be faithful like Jesus. Amen.

Sharing Our Good News

Before continuing, take a few moments to share with the group something of your experience of prayer since our last meeting, including anything that might have resulted from "Living the Good News."

Reflection 1

"I must be in my Father's house"

"At Milan station, I once saw a porter who, with his head resting on a sack of coal propped against a pillar, was sound asleep… Trains left whistling and arrived with clanking wheels; the loudspeakers continually boomed out announcements; people came and went in confusion and noise, but he—sleeping on—seemed to be saying: 'Do what you like, but I need to be quiet.' We priests should do something similar: around us there is continual movement and talking, of persons, newspapers, radio, and television. With priestly moderation and discipline we must say: 'Beyond certain limits, for me, who am a priest of the Lord, you do not exist. I must take a little silence for my soul. I detach myself from you to be united with my God.'"

Address of Pope John Paul I to the Roman Clergy, September 7, 1978

The spirit of the pope's advice to his fellow priests could benefit anyone seeking a life of prayer. We can learn about prayer most fully in the example of the life and ministry of Jesus who, as we shall see, often found it best to detach himself in order to be united with God. Jesus—who shared our human nature—was taught to pray by Mary, his mother, and Joseph, his foster father. As a boy growing in his Jewish faith, he was also taught the prayers of his people at the synagogue in Nazareth and the Temple in Jerusalem. But the intense prayer of Jesus that is described in the Gospels springs from his loving relationship with God. That Jesus was already aware of this at the age of 12 is implied by his remark: "I must be in my father's house" (*Lk* 2:49). And, in fact, Jesus repeatedly provides us with the perfect model of the prayer of a child toward a loving parent (*CCC*, 2599).

The Gospel according to Luke describes an important pattern in the prayer life of Jesus. He prays before decisive events in his ministry—for example, before the voice from heaven proclaimed him "my Son, the Beloved" after the baptism by John; before he called his apostles; before God declared him "my Son, my Chosen" during the Transfiguration; and before his passion and death (*Lk* 3:21-22; 6:12-16; 9:28; 22:41-44). Jesus' prayer before these critical times is a humble and trusting commitment of his human will to the will of God (*CCC*, 2600).

Sharing Question

- To what extent does all the "noise" in your world—inside and outside your home—keep you from prayer?

The following passage from the Gospel according to Mark suggests that those who sought Jesus' help, and even his closest friends, did not always understand his spiritual life:

Pondering the Word

"Everyone is searching for you"

Mark 1:32-37

Sharing Questions

- Take a moment to reflect on what word, phrase, or image from the scripture passage touches your heart or speaks to your life. Reflect in silence on your thoughts, or share them aloud.

- How does the reaction of co-workers, friends, and family members affect your prayer life?

Hold nothing back, pray without ceasing

Raïssa Oumansoff was born in Russia to an Orthodox Jewish family. Her parents moved the family to France to assure good schooling for Raïssa and her sister, Vera. Raïssa was admitted to study at the Sorbonne when she was 16 years old. There she met student Jacques Maritain, a Protestant, with whom she shared many interests, including philosophy. They were married in 1904 and after two years of inquiry they both were baptized as Catholics. Their faith grew so deep that they took the vows of the Oblates of St. Benedict and vows of perpetual chastity. Raïssa became a noted poet and philosopher, and Jacques became one of the leading Catholic philosophers of the 20th century. One of his great contributions was to "reintroduce" the Church to the philosophy of the 13th century theologian St. Thomas Aquinas—a pursuit that was inspired by Raïssa. After Raïssa's death in 1960, her husband discovered her private journals. These volumes revealed Raïssa's intense prayer life which she described this way:

"I have the feeling that what is asked of us is to live in the whirlwind, without keeping back any of our substance, without keeping back anything for ourselves, neither rest nor friendships nor health nor leisure—to pray incessantly ... in fact, to let ourselves pitch and toss in the waves of the divine will till the day when it will say: 'That's enough.'"

Reflection 2

"Lord, teach us to pray."

As his disciples watched and listened to Jesus, one of them said, "Lord, teach us to pray" (*Lk* 11:1). We, too, can learn from what Jesus did and what he said in prayer. First, it is clear throughout the Gospels that Jesus prayed constantly. He included in his prayer all people. In order to free his human sisters and brothers, Jesus—tested by the same weaknesses as ourselves—shares in his human prayer everything that we experience, except sin (Cf. *Heb* 2:12, 15; 4:15) (*CCC*, 2602). The Gospels show us, too, that Jesus began his prayers with thanksgiving, as he did before he called Lazarus from the tomb: "Father, I thank you for having heard me" (*Jn* 11:41-42). Significantly, Jesus thanked the Giver before the gift was received.

The prayer of Jesus expressed the total submission of his human heart to God's will—an example we are called to imitate. As his passion and death approached, even though he dreaded what was ahead of him, he prayed for the world and for those who would follow him (*Jn* 17). As for himself, he was steadfast in accepting the divine will, praying, even as death enveloped him: "Father, into your hands I commend my spirit" (*Lk* 23:46) (*CCC*, 2604-2606).

Besides teaching us by example, Jesus teaches us directly. Beginning with the Sermon on the Mount, Jesus called people to a conversion of heart that included reconciling with their sisters and brothers before bringing a sacrifice to the altar. He told people not to make a show of their prayer, but to pray in private; he told them not to think that prayer required a barrage of "empty phrases … for your Father knows what you need before you ask him" (*Mt* 6:7-8) (*CCC*, 2608-2609)

Jesus also teaches us to pray with the confidence of children trusting in their parents: "Whatever you ask for in prayer, believe that you have received it, and it will be yours" (*Mk* 11:24). In addition to conversion and faith, Jesus urged watchfulness, attentiveness to what God has done, to God's presence in the world, and to the promise that Christ will come again in glory. Jesus' instruction—"Stay awake" (*Mt* 26:41)—meant that always being at prayer is the only way to avoid falling into temptation (*CCC*, 2612).

As Jesus taught his disciples how to pray, he told them that once he was no longer physically with them, they would pray to God in Jesus' name. For us, as for the first disciples, that means that we can be confident that we will be heard when we pray, as we so often do, "through your son, Jesus Christ, our Lord" (Cf. *Jn* 14:13-14)" (*CCC*, 2614). Even more, when our prayer is united with the prayer of Jesus, God gives us the Holy Spirit, in whom "Christian prayer is a communion of love with the Father, not only through Christ but also in him" (*CCC*, 2615).

Our prayer is modeled also after the prayer of the Virgin Mary. Her response when the angel told her that she would bear a son was to completely embrace God's plan for her: "Let it be with me according to your word" (*Lk* 1:38). Mary's later expression of humility, joy, and thanksgiving—"My soul magnifies the Lord" (*Lk* 1:46-55)—became the prayer of the whole Church. At the wedding feast at Cana, she was revealed as the mediator who would intercede with her Son for us (*Jn* 2:1-12). Her selflessness continued at the foot of the cross, where she freely gave up her only Son for our salvation (*CCC*, 2617-2619), and when the Church, her son's Body, had been established, Mary was among the faithful who were "constantly devoting themselves to prayer" (*Acts* 1:14).

Spotlight on the *Catechism*

""In the Latin Church, the Rosary, a venerable and powerful form of prayer, developed out of popular piety. Praying the Rosary involves the recitation of vocal prayers, including the Our Father, the Hail Mary, and the Glory Be, while meditating on mysteries in the life of Jesus. In the Eastern Churches, litanies and hymns to the Mother of God are more commonly prayed.

"We do not pray to Mary in the same way we pray to God. In prayer to Mary, we invoke her intercession on behalf of our needs, whereas when we pray to God we ask him directly for gifts and favors."

United States Catholic Catechism for Adults, pp. 471-472

One of the most familiar prayers to Catholic Christians—"Hail Mary, full of grace"—expresses our desire to join the Blessed Mother in praising God for what he has done for her and, therefore, for us, and seeking her intercession. The prayer begins with the angel Gabriel's words, as recorded by St. Luke, words that mean that Mary "is a sinless woman, blessed with a deep union with God" (*USCCA*, p. 470). This union does not mean that Mary was set apart from us by being deprived of her free will; on the contrary, it means that she gave us example by freely entering with her whole heart into the friendship God offered her.

This prayer we call the "Hail Mary" or "Ave Maria" also repeats the greeting Mary received when she visited her cousin Elizabeth, who was to be the mother of John the Baptist: "Blessed are you among women, and blessed is the fruit of your womb" (*Lk* 1:42). Elizabeth here anticipated the prayers of generations of Christians who have made Mary the world's most honored woman and praised her for her faith (*USCCA*, pp. 470-471).

The second part of the prayer—"Holy Mary, Mother of God"—which was composed in the Middle Ages, proclaims Mary's proper title since her son, Jesus, was truly God and truly human. Then the prayer expresses our invocation, "pray for us sinners, now and at the hour of our death." Jesus is always interceding for us with our Creator, and he encourages us to intercede for each other. "The saints and the Blessed Virgin Mary continue this prayer of intercession in heaven. As Mother of the Church, Mary continues to pray with a mother's care for the Body of her Son on earth" (*USCCA*, p. 471). Mary makes this prayer after having made her own "pilgrimage of faith," accepting the will of God and facing the difficulties of life, including the persecution and death of her Son. "She knows what a journey of faith entails, and she accompanies us with prayer as we make our journey to God throughout our lives and at death" (*USCCA*, p. 471).

Sharing Questions

- Even when he was approaching death, Jesus accepted the will of God. Mary, his mother, also provided an example of faith as she embraced God's friendship despite the suffering in her life. Recall and share an occasion when you accepted God's will and left the outcome in his hands as you prayed for yourself or for someone else.

- How can you shuffle your routine to make prayer an even more prominent part of your daily life?

Living the Good News

Jesus emphasized the connection between faith and action, between what we believe and what we do. In that spirit, decide on an individual or group action that flows from what you have shared in this session. If you decide to act on your own, share your decision with the group. If you decide on a group action, determine among you which individual members will take responsibility for various aspects of the action.

You are likely to benefit most from taking an action that arises from your own response to the session. However, you can consider one of the following suggestions or use these ideas to help develop one of your own:

- Make a commitment to read one of the Gospels during the coming week.

- Set aside some time each day for quiet prayer.

- Pray the Magnificat (Luke 1:46-55) each day for all Church and civic leaders, praying that justice will be integral to their decisions.

As my response to the Gospel of Jesus, I commit to:

_____

_____

Lifting Our Hearts

Pray for a few minutes in silence. Then, pray together:

Leader	Christ be with us.
All	**Christ be with me, Christ within me, Christ behind me, Christ before me,**
Leader	Christ be with us.
All	**Christ beside me, Christ to win me, Christ to comfort me and restore me,**
Leader	Christ be with us.
All	**Christ beneath me, Christ above me, Christ in quiet, Christ in danger,**
Leader	Christ be with us.
All	**Christ in heart of all that love me, Christ in mouth of friend and stranger. Amen.**

The Breastplate of St. Patrick

Looking Ahead

- Prepare for your next session by prayerfully reading and studying:
    - Session 4: Expressions of Prayer;
    - Scripture: Ephesians 1:3-6 (A prayer in praise of God's plan of salvation);
    - pages 467-468 on "Prayer in the New Testament Church" from Chapter 35, "God Calls Us to Pray," in the *United States Catholic Catechism for Adults*;
    - paragraphs 2623-2649 in the *Catechism of the Catholic Church* on prayer in the age of the Church.
- Remember to use RENEWING FAMILY FAITH and its helpful suggestions on how to extend the fruits of your sharing beyond your group, especially to your families. See page 93.

Expressions of Prayer

Suggested Environment

Provide a basket, some small sheets of paper and some pens. As part of the opening prayer, ask group members to write prayer petitions on the papers and place them in the basket. As part of the closing prayer, invite everyone to take a prayer intention from the basket and pray for that intention during the following week. You may also have a Bible— open to the reading for this session—displayed on a small table along with a burning candle. Consider decorating the table with the color of the liturgical season and other symbols of faith.

In addition, it is helpful to have available the Catechism of the Catholic Church (CCC) *and the* United States Catholic Catechism for Adults (USCCA).

Begin with a quiet, reflective atmosphere.

Lifting Our Hearts

Song Suggestion

"Canticle of the Turning," Rory Cooney

Prayer

Pray together

Holy Trinity, one God,
as we gather again to share our faith,
we reflect on the many ways
we speak to you with the gift of prayer.

We bless and adore you because you have blessed us.
We ask you to forgive our failings and to provide for our needs.
We seek your help for those who are troubled.
We thank you for all you have done for our salvation.
We praise you, because you are most high,
the focus and goal of our lives.

We make our prayer to you through Jesus Christ in the unity of the Holy Spirit, one God forever and ever.

Amen.

Sharing Our Good News

Before continuing, take a few moments to share with the group something of your experience of prayer since our last meeting, including anything that may have resulted from "Living the Good News."

Reflection 1

Sacrament, charity, and prayer

Edith Stein took a fitful journey to faith in Jesus. One of her stops was at an historic Catholic church in Frankfurt, Germany. The scholar, who had been born to a Jewish family, was already inquiring into Christianity. Ultimately she would become not only a Catholic but a Carmelite nun, would die at the hands of the Nazis, and would be canonized St. Teresa Benedicta of the Cross. But she was only a tourist in the Frankfurt church when she saw a woman with a shopping basket come in to pray before the tabernacle. Edith Stein later wrote that she had never seen such a thing in a house of worship—a person taking time, in the middle of the day, to have a conversation with God. Pope John Paul II canonized Edith Stein in 1998.

Sharing Question

• Recall a time when you spontaneously "dropped everything" on a busy day in order to spend a few moments with God in prayer.

A woman like the one who amazed Edith Stein might not have seemed unusual to the early Christian community. Prayer has been central to the life of the Church from the very beginning. In fact, St. Luke tells us that even before Pentecost, the apostles joined other followers of Jesus in constant prayer and that, once the Holy Spirit had been poured out on the disciples, those who flocked to join the Christian community in Jerusalem "devoted themselves to the apostles' teaching and the fellowship, to the breaking of bread and the prayers" (*Acts* 2:42). In other words, they entered into the pattern that still characterizes the prayer life of the Church: founded on the faith handed down by the apostles, practiced in the charity that Jesus preached and lived, and fed and sustained by the Eucharist (CCC, 2623-2624).

Beginning in the time of the apostles, the prayer life of the Church has been rooted in the Scriptures and, as we have seen, especially in the Psalms. The Holy Spirit has also inspired the Church to develop new forms of prayer—always in keeping with the Scriptures and with apostolic tradition. The *Catechism of the Catholic Church* focuses on five forms of prayer for which the Church provides guidance: blessing and adoration, petition, intercession, thanksgiving, and praise.

Sharing Question

• How do you pray most often—by reciting traditional prayers, by spontaneous vocal prayer, by silent prayer? Why does that mode of prayer appeal to you?

Pondering the Word

Blessing the God who blesses us

Ephesians: 1:3-6

Sharing Questions

• Take a moment to reflect on what word, phrase, or image from the scripture passage touches your heart or speaks to your life. Reflect in silence on your thoughts, or share them aloud.

• Normally, we think of God blessing us. What has happened in your life that might prompt you to bless God as St. Paul does in his prayer?

Spotlight on the *Catechism*

"The infant Church was born in prayer, lived in prayer, and thrived in prayer …

The letters of St. Paul show him to be a man of intense prayer. Throughout his Letters, there are prayers of praise to God for blessings the Church and he himself have received. There are also prayers of intercession as he seeks God's grace for the communities he has evangelized. And he describes his own personal prayers to God, especially in times of difficulty."

Adapted from *United States Catholic Catechism for Adults*, p. 467

Reflection 2

Prayers of blessing and adoration

Prayers of blessing and adoration flow from our awareness of God's love for us. We express our wonder at what God has created. We acknowledge what God has done for us as a people down through the ages and in our personal lives. The prayer of blessing is our response to God's gifts: because we recognize and acknowledge what God has done for us, we in turn bless God as the source of all that is good in our lives (*CCC*, 2626). Underlying this dialogue is adoration, in which we both respect and exalt the greatness of our creator and the power of Jesus Christ, who saved us from the consequences of sin and death (*CCC*, 2628).

> We come into the world
> Not to be admired
> Not to be understood
> Not to worry.
>
> We are here
> To have our soul kneeling
> And our eyes wide open
> In absolute amazement before God.
>
> —Irma Chávez
> (Salvadoran poet and evangelizer)

Offer spontaneous prayers of blessing and adoration, acknowledging what God has done for humanity and for you personally.

Prayer of petition

Petition is one of the most familiar forms of prayer. We often say to God, "This is what I need." We acknowledge both that we depend on God for our very existence and for all that we have, and that we have turned away from him in sin (*CCC*, 2629). Although the mention of petition might suggest material needs—or simply material desires—the *Catechism* reminds us that we should always pray first for God to forgive our sins (*CCC*, 2631). In fact, this primary petition, this expression of trusting humility, is a prerequisite for both personal prayer and for the celebration of the Eucharist (*CCC*, 2631).

The object of our petitions should be, as Jesus taught, the desire for and the search for the Reign of God. We pray first for the Kingdom and then "for what is necessary to welcome it and cooperate with its coming" (*CCC*, 2632). In other words, we pray for the vision and strength to do God's will so that we collaborate with the Son and the Holy Spirit in establishing more fully the Reign of God in the world. Therefore, every need can become the object of our petition when we share in, cooperate with, God's saving love (*CCC*, 2830). That's what we so often pray for, as Jesus taught us: "Your will be done, on earth as it is in heaven" (*Mt* 6:10).

Pause for a moment to consider what you most need from God, including forgiveness and reconciliation, and then offer spontaneous prayers of petition.

Prayer of intercession

Intercession is prayer on behalf of another. In this form, we imitate the Son, who prayed on earth for his disciples, and who now is the one who intercedes with God on our behalf (*Jn* 17:9-10; 1 *Jn* 2:1) (*CCC*, 2634). Since Abraham interceded on behalf of the innocent of Sodom and Gomorrah, this form of prayer has been practiced by men and women who trust in the mercy of God (*CCC*, 2635). The first Christian communities practiced intercession as an expression of the fellowship they lived intensely (cf. *Acts* 12:5; 20:36; 21:5; 2 *Cor* 9:14). Like them, we recognize our call to pray for one another; we do so in private, in the Mass, and in *The Liturgy of the Hours*. We pray for all people, for our entire world. We pray for those we love and those we find difficult to love. We pray for those who care for us and those who do us harm (*CCC*, 2636; *USCCA*, p. 468).

Offer spontaneous prayers of intercession for others, including those with whom you struggle or disagree.

Prayer of thanksgiving

Whatever God gives us, whatever we ask of him, we are called to respond to him in thanksgiving. Indeed, God has given us a Savior, and the name of the sacrament—the Eucharist—in which the Savior is intimately present to us *means* thanksgiving; the Church's prayer as she celebrates that sacrament is characterized by thanksgiving (*CCC*, 2637).

St. Paul urged Christians to continuously give thanks to God, and he set an example with his own life. It is typical of his letters that he prominently offers thanks for what God has done in his life and in the early Christian community (*CCC*, 2638). "Every moment or event can become a thanksgiving offering. We are called to thank God for all the gifts we have received, including our joys and sorrows, all of which, through love, work towards our benefit" (*USCCA*, p. 468).

Take a few moments to reflect on something for which you are grateful. Offer spontaneous prayers of thanksgiving.

Prayer of praise

We praise God in prayer not because of what he has done, but just because he is—he exists. When we praise God, we join with his Spirit to bear witness to the fact that we are God's children who love him now in faith, and hope to see him "face to face" in heaven. Praise is the prayer form that embraces all the others and focuses them on the source and goal of all prayer: God (*CCC*, 2639). United with all the saints and angels, as members of the Church on earth, we sing songs of praise with faith in a God who loves us beyond all imagining (*CCC*, 2642).

As a group, pray the "Holy, Holy, Holy" from the Mass, and then follow it with spontaneous prayers of praise to God.

Sharing Questions

• What events or experiences affecting you or others have prompted you to praise God or pray to him in thanksgiving? What events do

The Church prays ceaselessly in
The Liturgy of the Hours

When the Church was first taking form as a network of small communities, Christians continued the Jewish practice of praying at appointed times in the day and night in order to make holy the whole day and all human activity. This practice evolved into what is now known as *The Liturgy of the Hours* or Divine Office. While this prayer was once practiced mostly by clergy and religious orders, it has become increasingly popular with the laity.

The Liturgy of the Hours consists of specific psalms, scriptural and non-scriptural readings, prayers, and hymns prescribed for each day of the week. In its present form, which was approved in 1970 by Pope Paul VI, *The Liturgy of the Hours* is divided into Morning Prayer, or Lauds; Daytime Prayer, which can include brief prayers at mid-morning, midday, and mid-afternoon; Evening Prayer, or Vespers; and Night Prayer, or Compline. In addition, the Office of Readings may be prayed at any time.

The Liturgy of the Hours may be prayed privately or in groups. The prayer is published in book form—it is often referred to as the Breviary—and a guide for each day's prayer is published each year. Anyone who wishes to pray *The Liturgy of the Hours* for the first time should seek guidance from someone who is familiar with its organization, which reflects the liturgical seasons as well as feast days and other observances on given days of the year.

The Church is ceaselessly "praising the Lord and interceding for the salvation of the whole world. She does this, not only by celebrating the Eucharist, but also in other ways, especially by praying the divine office" (*Constitution on the Sacred Liturgy*, 83), and she encourages us to add our voices.

you look forward to that might be the subject of prayers of praise and thanksgiving?

• What new mode of prayer are you willing to try based on your experience in this session? Why are you attracted to that new form of prayer?

Living the Good News

Jesus emphasized the connection between faith and action, between what we believe and what we do. In that spirit, decide on an individual or group action that flows from what you have shared in this session. If you decide to act on your own, share your decision with the group. If you decide on a group action, determine among you which individual members will take responsibility for various aspects of the action.

You are likely to benefit most from taking an action that arises from your own response to the session. However, you can consider one of the following suggestions or use these ideas to help develop one of your own:

• Keep a prayer journal and write various forms of prayer to God.

• Take a walk in nature and offer prayers of praise to God for the beauty of creation.

• Make a list of things you can do to thank God for his creation by caring for it better or by encouraging others to do so.

As my response to the Gospel of Jesus, I commit to:

_____

_____

Lifting Our Hearts

Pray Psalm 103, a psalm of David. Individual group members take turns reading each "Voice."

All   **Bless the Lord, O my soul,**
      and all that is within me,
      bless his holy name.

      Bless the Lord, O my soul,
      and do not forget all his benefits—'
    who forgives all your iniquity,
      who heals all your diseases,
      who redeems your life from the Pit,

who crowns you with steadfast love and mercy,
who satisfies you with good as long as you live
so that your youth is renewed like the eagle's.

Voice   The Lord works vindication
               and justice for all who are oppressed.

Voice   He made known his ways to Moses,
               his acts to the people of Israel.

Voice   The Lord is merciful and gracious,
               slow to anger and abounding in steadfast love.

Voice   He will not always accuse,
               nor will he keep his anger forever.

Voice   He does not deal with us according to our sins,
               nor repay us according to our iniquities.

Voice   For as the heavens are high above the earth,
               so great is his steadfast love towards those who fear him;
           as far as the east is from the west,
               so far he removes our transgressions from us.

Voice   As a father has compassion for his children,
               so the Lord has compassion for those who fear him.

Voice   For he knows how we were made;
               he remembers that we are dust.

Voice   As for mortals, their days are like grass;
               they flourish like a flower of the field;
           for the wind passes over it, and it is gone,
               and its place knows it no more.

Voice   But the steadfast love of the Lord
           is from everlasting to everlasting
               on those who fear him,
               and his righteousness to children's children,
           to those who keep his covenant
               and remember to do his commandments.

Voice   The Lord has established his throne in the heavens,
               and his kingdom rules over all.

All   **Bless the Lord, O you his angels,**
               you mighty ones who do his bidding,
               obedient to his spoken word.

> **Bless the Lord, all his hosts,**
> **his ministers that do his will.**
>
> **Bless the Lord, all his works,**
> **in all places of his dominion.**
> **Bless the Lord, O my soul.**
>
> **Amen.**

Looking Ahead

- Prepare for your next session by prayerfully reading and studying:
  - Session 5: The Sources and Ways of Prayer;
  - Matthew 6:5-8 (Jesus' teaching about prayer);
  - pages 468-469 on "The Sources and Manner of Praying" from the *United States Catholic Catechism for Adults*, Chapter 35, "God Calls Us to Pray";
  - paragraphs 2650-2682 of the *Catechism of the Catholic Church*, which explore the Christian tradition of prayer: "At the Wellsprings of Prayer" and "The Way of Prayer."

- Remember to use RENEWING FAMILY FAITH and its helpful suggestions on how to extend the fruits of your sharing beyond your group, especially to your families. See page 93.

The Sources and Ways of Prayer

Suggested Environment

You may have a Bible—open to the reading for this session—displayed on a small table along with a burning candle. Near the Bible, place a simple sign with the one word "Jesus." Consider decorating the table with the color of the liturgical season and other symbols of faith.

In addition, it is helpful to have available the Catechism of the Catholic Church (CCC) *and the* United States Catholic Catechism for Adults (USCCA).

Begin with a quiet, reflective atmosphere.

Lifting Our Hearts

Song Suggestion

"We Are Called," David Haas

Prayer

Pray together

Ever-present God,
we come together to reflect on our faith
because we are a people of prayer.

We ask you in your Holy Spirit
to help us make our prayer
an ever-growing, ever-deepening
part of our daily lives
as we read and meditate on your word,
praise and thank you in the Eucharist,
and return to you again and again
through the hours of our days.

We ask all this in the holy name of Jesus.

Amen.

Sharing Our Good News

Before continuing, take a few moments to share with the group something of your experience of prayer since our last meeting, including anything that might have resulted from "Living the Good News."

Reflection 1

Praying with faith, hope, and love

Jean-Marie Vianney's journey to a place among the saints got off to an inauspicious start. When he was four, all the churches in France were closed by the "reign of terror" following the French Revolution, and priests celebrated Mass at his family's farm under cover of night. The boy we now know as St. John Vianney pursued his own prayers in the hollow of a tree. Because of his duties on the farm, he was uneducated until he was 17, and when he did go to school, he was a slow student. He had his mind on the priesthood; instead, he was drafted into Napoleon's army but ended up in the company of deserters, at times hiding in haystacks to avoid the gendarmes. He was 29 before he finally was ordained. He was assigned to a neglected parish in the obscure village of Ars, and there his enormous charity and self-denial, along with his preaching and his devotion to the sacrament of penance, made him a reluctant celebrity throughout France. He died in 1859 and was canonized in 1925.

Sharing Question

• As a boy, St. John Vianney went off by himself to pray. What is your earliest memory of prayer?

St. John Vianney was taught to pray—and did pray—from childhood. His life of devotion despite difficulties dramatized the fact that prayer does not just happen; nor can prayer be reduced to spur-of-the-moment expressions of inner impulses. Rather, we must have the will to pray—we must pray deliberately—and we must *learn* to pray. With respect to learning, we are not left on our own. The Holy Spirit teaches us prayer through the legacy—the Sacred Tradition—that is handed down to us in the Church (*CCC*, 2650). That tradition continues to grow as members of the Church contemplate the events and written proclamations of salvation and share the spiritual realities in their own lives (*CCC*, 2651). In addition, we learn to pray by reflecting on the great gifts God has given us, especially the gifts of creation and grace.

We also learn to pray by reading and reflecting on the Scriptures, by celebrating the sacramental liturgy of the Church, and by practicing the theological virtues—faith, hope, and love.

With regard to Scripture, the Church urges us read God's Word frequently in order to increase our knowledge of Jesus, but she reminds us to accompany our reading with prayer so that we carry on a dialogue with God. We speak to God when we pray, and we listen to God when we read his Word in the sacred texts (*CCC*, 2653).

Christ and the Holy Spirit proclaim the mystery of our salvation and make it present to us in the celebration of the sacraments. When we pray, we "take in" the sacramental liturgy, make it a part of us. That prayer—which is the prayer of the Church even when we practice it in private—continues in our hearts even after the celebration (*CCC*, 2655). Dorothy Day, co-founder of the Catholic Worker movement, described the effect of liturgy in her own life as a champion of the poor: "Living the liturgical day as much as we are able … . we find that it is now not us, but Christ in us, who is working to combat injustice and oppression. We are on our way to becoming 'other Christs.' "

We pray and we celebrate liturgy because we have *faith* in God's presence among us. The Holy Spirit prompts us to celebrate

Spotlight on the *Catechism*

"St. Paul calls us to 'pray without ceasing' (1 *Thes* 5:17). The will to pray in a daily, sustained, and structured manner is essential for becoming a prayerful person. The Holy Spirit guides the Church at prayer through her reading of Scripture, her celebration of the liturgy, and the practice of faith, hope and love.

By our active participation in the liturgy, the prayer of the Church, we encounter the Father, and the Son, and the Holy Spirit, who impart to us the gifts of salvation. Spiritual writers tell us our heart can be an altar of adoration and praise. Prayer internalizes the liturgy both during and after its celebration.

Faith puts vitality in prayer because it brings us to a personal relationship with Christ. Hope carries our prayer to our final goal of permanent union with God. Love, poured into our heart by the Holy Spirit, is the source and destiny of prayer."

United States Catholic Catechism for Adults, pp. 468-69

liturgy expecting the return of Christ, and to pray with that *hope*. "Conversely, the prayer of the Church and personal prayer nourish hope in us" (*CCC*, 2657). Our hope is not in vain, because the Holy Spirit has poured God's love into our hearts (*CCC*, 2658).

We learn to pray at certain times and places, including in our celebration of the Eucharist, but the Spirit of God is offered to us all day every day. We encounter God in the present, not yesterday or tomorrow. We are right to petition God to intervene in major world events—war, political or economic oppression, natural disaster—but we are also right to call on God's help in the problems of everyday life (*CCC*, 2660). St. Louise de Marillac, who co-founded the Daughters of Charity in 17th-century France, encouraged the sisters to pray and work at the same time, asking themselves as they moved from task to task, "What would Jesus do?"

Sharing Question

• How does your relationship with God allow you to pray for peace, justice, and healing in the midst of personal problems or crises in the world?

Pondering the Word

"Go into your room and pray"

Matthew 6:5-8

Sharing Questions

• Take a moment to reflect on what word, phrase, or image from the scripture passage touches your heart or speaks to your life. Reflect in silence on your thoughts, or share them aloud.

• How and when have you learned to pray?

Reflection 2

The Holy Name

The Holy Spirit teaches us to pray through the sacred humanity of Jesus. In fact, the *only* way of Christian prayer—whether it's communal or personal, vocal or interior—is through Jesus (*CCC*, 2664). This is reflected in the liturgy of the Church with its many prayers addressed to Jesus Christ (*CCC*, 2665). The name of Jesus in itself is the simplest of all prayers.

As a group, spend ten minutes in quiet reflection. Each person closes his or her eyes and relaxes. The leader asks the members of the group to breathe in the calm that comes with awareness of God's presence and breathe out all their cares and worries. Then each person is invited to slowly and silently repeat the name of Jesus over and over for ten minutes.

Sharing Question

• Your group has just prayed by using only the name of Jesus. What was that experience like for you?

Reflection 3

"Fill the hearts of your faithful"

Any time we pray to Jesus, it is the Holy Spirit who has prompted us. In fact, St. Paul wrote, "no one can say 'Jesus is Lord' except by the Holy Spirit" (1 *Cor* 12:3). So, the *Catechism* asks, since the Holy Spirit teaches us to pray to the Son, "how could we not pray to the Spirit too? That is why the Church invites us to call upon the Holy Spirit every day" (*CCC*, 2670), especially before and after every important action we take. There are prayers and hymns to the Holy Spirit in every Christian liturgical tradition, East and West (*CCC*, 2671), but it is the one Spirit who acts in each of us (*CCC*, 2672).

> # Praise Jesus' name "at all times"
>
> St. Bernardine of Siena, a 15th-century Franciscan friar, was tireless in promoting devotion to the name of Jesus. He held up the Apostle Paul as an example to Christians: "By word of mouth, by letters, by miracles and by the example of his own life, St. Paul bore the name of Jesus wherever he went. He praised the name of Jesus at all times, but never more than when bearing witness to his faith."

Take a few minutes as a group to pray the following prayers for the power of the Spirit. Pray each line slowly and reflectively, pausing between the two prayers.

Come, Holy Spirit, fill the hearts of your faithful; and kindle in them the fire of your love.

Pentecost Sequence, Roman Missal

Heavenly King, Consoler Spirit, Spirit of Truth, present everywhere and filling all things, treasure of all good and source of all life,

come dwell in us, cleanse and save us,
you who are All Good.

Byzantine Liturgy, Pentecost Vespers

Sharing Question

• Do you often address your prayer to God, the Holy Spirit? In what circumstances would you pray in that way?

Reflection 4

Prayer inspired by Mary

We reflected in Session 3 on how Mary consistently embraced the will of God, from the Annunciation to the death of Jesus, setting an example that inspires our own prayer. Ever since then, Mary has been the mother of all Christians, and, as our mother, she shows us the way to him. Prayer to Mary that has developed over the ages is usually expressed in two themes. The first "magnifies" the Lord for the "great things" he did for Mary and, through her, for all human beings; the second entrusts all our cares and petitions to her (CCC, 2675). "By entrusting ourselves to her prayer, we abandon ourselves to the will of God together with her…" (CCC, 2677).

Sharing Question

• Mary has a relationship to God that no other human being shares. As much as she is set apart in that way, why do many people find prayer to Mary attractive and comforting?

Living the Good News

Jesus emphasized the connection between faith and action, between what we believe and what we do. In that spirit, decide on an individual or group action that flows from what you have shared in this session. If you decide to act on your own, share your decision with the group. If you decide on a group action, determine among you which individual members will take responsibility for various aspects of the action.

You are likely to benefit most from taking an action that arises from your own response to the session. However, you can consider one of the following suggestions or use these ideas to help develop one of your own:

- Make notes in your journal about what happened during your daily prayer.

- Pray for ten minutes daily in the manner described at the top of page 39.

- Pray to the Holy Spirit for the needs of the world. As you learn the news of each day, ask the Holy Spirit to bring God's power into painful situations.

As my response to the Gospel of Jesus, I commit to:

_____

_____

Lifting Our Hearts

Offer spontaneous prayers expressing faith, hope, or love.

Pray together

Leader	Almighty God, we pray in church and at home and as we go about our daily lives because we have faith that you are with us in all places and at all times.
All	**We pray for ourselves and for others that we will some day be united with you because we have hope in the promises you have made through your Son, Jesus Christ.**
	We pray without fear or discouragement always open to your divine will because of the love that sustains us as a gift of your most Holy Spirit.
Leader	We offer our prayer through Jesus Christ, your Son in the unity of the Holy Spirit, one God forever and ever.
All	**Amen.**

Looking Ahead

- Prepare for your next session by prayerfully reading and studying:

  - Session 6: Guides for Prayer;

  - Scripture: 1 Thessalonians 1:2-10 (Paul's prayer of thanksgiving for the faith and good works of the Thessalonians);

  - *United States Catholic Catechism for Adults*, Chapter 35, "God Calls Us to Pray": "Guides for Prayer" on p. 472 and "Pray Always (1 *Thes* 5:17)" on pp. 476-477;

  - paragraphs 2683-2696 on "Guides for Prayer" of the *Catechism of the Catholic Church*.

- Remember to use RENEWING FAMILY FAITH and its helpful suggestions on how to extend the fruits of your sharing beyond your group, especially to your families. See page 93.

Guides for Prayer

Suggested Environment

You may have a Bible—open to the reading for this session—displayed on a small table along with a burning candle. Near the Bible, you may place the names or pictures of people such as Jesus, Mary, St. Paul, St. Ignatius Loyola, and Pope John Paul II, who have been guides for us in prayer. Consider decorating the table with the color of the liturgical season and other symbols of faith.

In addition, it is helpful to have available the Catechism of the Catholic Church (CCC) *and the* United States Catholic Catechism for Adults (USCCA).

Begin with a quiet, reflective atmosphere.

Lifting Our Hearts

Song Suggestion

"Glory and Praise to our God," Daniel L. Schutte

Prayer

Pray together

Ever-present God,
as we gather to share our faith
help us to grow ever closer to you
not only here and now
but throughout our daily lives.

Help us to use the free will and understanding
that you have given us as gifts
to learn your will through prayer and reflection,
following the example of Jesus, his Blessed Mother,
and all the saints.

We ask this in the name of our Lord, Jesus Christ.

Amen.

Sharing Our Good News

Before continuing, take a few moments to share with the group something of your experience of prayer since our last meeting, including anything that may have resulted from "Living the Good News."

Reflection 1

All you saints, pray for us

Danny Thomas was one of the most successful figures in American entertainment in the mid 20th century: comedian, actor, singer, producer. It was a tough climb from a poor neighborhood in Toledo, and when his career was foundering Thomas, a Catholic, asked St. Jude Thaddeus to help him find his way in life. Thomas promised, in return, to build a shrine to the apostle. When Thomas had "made it" in show business, he founded St. Jude Children's Research Hospital in Memphis, Tenn., a pediatric cancer research center where children are treated regardless of their families' ability to pay. As a result of the answer to Danny Thomas's prayer, thousands of children are treated at St. Jude each year, and many more are helped by the research conducted there.

Sharing Question

• Recall an occasion when you asked one of the saints to intercede with God for you or another person.

The saints lived at particular times and places in the past, but they can guide and help us in the present by the example of their lives, by the content of their writings, and by their prayer. Whether their earthly lives ended in the 1st century or the 21st, their spirits endure: they live in God's presence and constantly praise him, and they continue to care for us. As Danny Thomas did with St. Jude, "We can and should ask them to intercede for us and for the whole world" (*CCC*, 2683).

Some of these saintly men and women, at different times in our Church's history, were instrumental in developing various modes of spirituality such as Benedictine, Franciscan, Dominican, Jesuit, ascetical, and charismatic. Each of these schools of spirituality is a part of the Church's tradition of prayer, and each provides its unique guide for the spiritual life. Each shows a different facet of the "one pure light of the Holy Spirit" (*CCC*, 2684).

Sharing Question

• What is it about a particular saint that attracts you or speaks to your life?

Pondering the Word

"You received the word with joy"

1 Thessalonians 1:2-10

Sharing Questions

• Take a moment to reflect on what word, phrase, or image from the scripture passage touches your heart or speaks to your life. Reflect in silence on your thoughts, or share them aloud.

• Paul compliments the Christians in Thessalonica because, after receiving the word of God from Paul and his companions, they had not kept it to themselves but spread it through the example of their prayerful lives and their good works. How do you imitate these biblical saints in your life?

Reflection 2

"Prayer is the life of the new heart"

There are many places where we receive guidance in prayer, whether "place" means a physical location, a community, or a personal or pastoral relationship. The first of these "places" is the family. A family that is founded on the sacrament of marriage is the "domestic church." Within the family, children first learn to pray,

> ## "Where they are gathered, I am there"
>
> "'For where two or three are gathered in my name, I am there among them' (*Mt* 18:20). This Letter to Families wishes in the first place to be a prayer to Christ to remain in every human family; an invitation to him, in and through the small family of parents and children, to dwell in the great family of nations, so that together with him all of us can truly say: 'Our Father'! ... Prayer increases the strength and spiritual unity of the family, helping the family to partake of God's own 'strength'. In the solemn nuptial blessing during the Rite of Marriage, the celebrant calls upon the Lord in these words: 'Pour out upon them the grace of the Holy Spirit so that by your love poured into their hearts they will remain faithful in the marriage covenant'. This 'visitation' of the Holy Spirit gives rise to the inner strength of families, as well as the power capable of uniting them in love and truth."
>
> Pope John Paul II, *Letter to Families*, No. 4

faithfully and persistently, as part of the *larger* family, the Church (*CCC*, 2685). Parents are called to teach their children to pray daily—to pray before meals and before going to bed, to pray for those who are sick, to pray for everyday needs, and to pray in gratitude and praise for God's gifts. In addition, couples and friends can strengthen their relationships by committing themselves to pray together regularly.

Of course, we also receive guidance in prayer in multiple ways within the Church itself. Ordained ministers are responsible, through instruction and example, for fostering the prayer lives of the faithful. Members of religious orders devote their time to both praising God and interceding with him on our behalf, providing a model for spiritual life. Catechists teach children and adults to meditate on God's Word in personal prayer, practice it in the liturgy, and keep it alive in their hearts at all times (*CCC*, 2686-2688).

One sign of renewal in the Church since the Second Vatican Council has been the emergence of prayer groups—what the *Catechism* calls "schools of prayer"—in which the faithful commit themselves to gather regularly to pray, to reflect together on the Scriptures, and to find ways to live their faith in everyday lives (*CCC*, 2689).

Another sign of renewal is the growing interest in spiritual direction or accompaniment (*CCC*, 2690). In this process, a trained spiritual companion helps a person hear with increasing clarity what God is personally communicating and then respond to God's voice both in prayer and in everyday living. The companion may be clergy, religious, or laity. Although such companions or guides are often called spiritual "directors," their function is not to direct in the sense of telling a person what to do. Spiritual direction is also not counseling. Its purpose is not to solve problems but to help a person find and respond to God in both the placid and the turbulent times of life. Spiritual direction aims to foster a more open and intimate relationship with God expressed in more open and intimate prayer. Those in search of a spiritual director can request a list from their diocese or parish.

We can pray anywhere, but some places are especially suitable for prayer. A church, first of all, is the proper place for a parish community to celebrate liturgy. A church "is also the privileged place for adoration of the real presence of Christ in the Blessed Sacrament" (*CCC*, 2691). Monasteries and retreat centers can provide the quiet atmosphere needed for deeper personal prayer, and shrines that are the focus of pilgrimages provide opportunities for "renewal in prayer" (Cf. *Presbyterorum ordinis* 7). Finally, an important place for prayer is the home. It can be helpful to set aside a small "prayer corner" with a Bible or icons or other signs that will mark that space as sacred and encourage regular prayer by individuals and by the family together (*CCC*, 2691).

"Prayer is the life of the new heart" (*CCC*, 2697). Prayer should enliven us at all times, but "we tend to forget him who is our all" (*CCC*, 2697). We cannot be always at prayer unless we first find specific times to pray. Our spiritual traditions have urged us to make daily practices, such as morning and evening prayer, grace before and after meals, *The Liturgy of the Hours,* and most important, Sunday Eucharist, primary times for prayer. If we want to grow in our love relationship with God, it is important for us to set aside some time each day to communicate our love and our desire for "new hearts" (*CCC*, 2697-2698).

Sharing Question

- How has your definition of prayer and your practice of prayer changed during the course of your life?

Spending time in his presence

A form of prayer that has enjoyed a revival in recent years is adoration of the Blessed Sacrament—that is, the Eucharist. Individual worshippers may engage in this form of prayer simply by spending time before the tabernacle where the Eucharist is reserved. However, many parishes set aside specific times for adoration; at those times, the Eucharist may be exposed to view, either in a ciborium or in a monstrance—an elaborate vessel made for that purpose. Adoration may be silent or it may be expressed in individual or communal prayer. Pope John Paul II, in a very personal way, encouraged this devotion to Christ: "It is pleasant to spend time with him, to lie close to his breast like the Beloved Disciple (cf. *Jn* 13:25) and to feel the infinite love present in his heart.... How often, dear brothers and sisters, have I experienced this, and drawn from it strength, consolation and support!"

Pope John Paul II, *Ecclesia de Eucharistia*

Living the Good News

Jesus emphasized the connection between faith and action, between what we believe and what we do. In that spirit, decide on an individual or group action that flows from what you have shared in this session. If you decide to act on your own, share your decision with the group. If you decide on a group action, determine among you which individual members will take responsibility for various aspects of the action.

You are likely to benefit most from taking an action that arises from your own response to the session. However, you can consider one of the following suggestions or use these ideas to help develop one of your own:

- Inquire in your parish about future retreats. Register, and invite a friend to go along.
- Create a prayer corner in your home.
- Consider what steps you could propose to encourage prayer before the Blessed Sacrament in your parish.
- Begin the practice in your home of praying the rosary as a family.
- Between seasons of *Why Catholic?* You may want to use the appropriate cycle of PRAYERTIME: *Faith-Sharing Reflections on the Sunday* Gospels, Cycle A, B, or C before every parish meeting (see page 95).

As my response to the Gospel of Jesus, I commit to:

_____

_____

Lifting Our Hearts

Take a few moments to reflect on a saint who has inspired you or helped you in some way. Offer a spontaneous prayer to that saint to intercede on your behalf, on behalf of your family or friends, or on behalf of this faith-sharing group.

Pray together.

All you saints in heaven, we honor you for your holy lives as we try to imitate your patience, your generosity, your faithfulness, and your courage. By striving through our prayer to become ever closer to God, we hope to be united with him and you forever, through Christ Our Lord. Amen.

Looking Ahead

- Prepare for your next session by prayerfully reading and studying:
  - Session 7: Vocal Prayer and Meditation;
  - Scripture: Mark 10:46-52 (Jesus heals Bartimaeus of his blindness);

- Chapter 18, pp. 234-247, "Sacrament of Penance and Reconciliation: God is Rich in Mercy" in the *United States Catholic Catechism for Adults;*

- paragraphs 2670-2704 and paragraph 2722 on vocal prayer and paragraphs 2705-2708 and 2723 on meditation in the *Catechism of the Catholic Church.*

• Remember to use *Renewing Family Faith* and its helpful suggestions on how to extend the fruits of your sharing beyond your group, especially to your families. See page 93.

Vocal Prayer and Meditation

Suggested Environment

You may have a Bible—open to the reading for this session—displayed on a small table along with a burning candle. With the Bible, you may display a worn-out coat or jacket or an old, coarse blanket. Consider decorating the table with colors of the liturgical season and other symbols of faith.

In addition, it is helpful to have available the Catechism of the Catholic Church (CCC) *and the* United States Catholic Catechism for Adults (USCCA).

Begin with a quiet, reflective atmosphere.

Lifting Our Hearts

Song Suggestion

"O, Lord, Hear My Prayer," Taizé

Prayer

Ever-present God,
as we gather to share our faith,
we thank you for giving us voices
with which we praise you,
and we thank you for giving us minds
with which we contemplate your word
and apply it to our lives.

We ask you in your Holy Spirit
to help us open ourselves
to pray with all of our faculties,
in the busy times and the quiet,
aloud and in silence,
as we grow ever closer to you.

We ask this through Jesus Christ, our Lord.

Amen.

Sharing Our Good News

Before continuing, take a few moments to share with the group something of your experience of prayer since our last meeting, including anything that might have resulted from "Living the Good News."

Reflection 1

Our words give voice to our hearts

Sister Thea Bowman, granddaughter of a slave, was an African-American born in Mississippi in 1937. She converted to Catholicism at an early age and joined the Franciscan Sisters of the Perpetual Adoration of La Crosse, Wisconsin. Sister Thea was a teacher at the elementary, secondary, and university levels, and she made scores of public appearances every year, encouraging cross-cultural understanding. In her talks and in her writing, she often attributed her faith and her spirituality to the influence of people she knew as a child. "God was so alive in my world," she wrote. "I was reared around a lot of old people. They knew Scripture. I knew people who could not read or write, but they could quote you a Scripture with the chapter and verse. They would use Scripture when they were tired and a Scripture when they were frustrated, a Scripture to challenge us … a Scripture to threaten you, a Scripture to reward you or to praise you or to teach you; I grew up in that kind of world."

Thea Bowman: *In My Own Words.*

Sharing Questions

• How did you begin reading the Bible?

• How do you integrate God's Word in the Scripture into your everyday life?

Christian tradition includes three major expressions of prayer: vocal, meditative, and contemplative. In this session we will focus on vocal prayer and meditation, and in Session 8 we will focus on contemplation.

Praying aloud has always been an important part of Christian worship (*CCC*, 2701). Jesus taught this way of speaking to God when he responded to his disciples' request: "Teach us to pray" (*Lk* 11:1). Jesus himself prayed aloud in the synagogue and in other circumstances mentioned explicitly in the Gospels (Cf. *Mt* 11:25-26; *Mk* 14:36) (*CCC*, 2701). Jesus warned that using many words does not

Spotlight on the *Catechism*

"Since we are body as well as spirit, we need to express ourselves orally. Spoken and sung prayers arise from our souls; they can be complemented by bodily gestures such as the Sign of the Cross, genuflection, kneeling, and bowing. When we become inwardly aware of God, to whom we speak, our vocal prayer can become an initial step toward contemplative prayer."

United States Catholic Catechism for Adults, p. 473

in itself necessarily constitute sincere and effective prayer (*Mt* 6:7-8), and St. John Chrysostom cautioned, "Whether or not our prayer is heard depends not on the number of words, but on the fervor of our souls" (St. John Chrysostom, *Ecloga de oratione* 2: PG 63, 585) (*CCC*, 2700). Still, the *Catechism* explains, vocal prayer is a requirement of our human nature: We are body and spirit, and we often feel the need to say aloud what we are feeling inside. The *Catechism* also points out that God wants vocal prayer from us because it involves our bodies and our minds together. We pray with our whole selves, which is the perfect honor we owe him (*CCC*, 2702-2703). As we pray outwardly, we became more deeply aware within ourselves of the God we are addressing (*CCC*, 2704).

Vocal prayer can be either prayer that we have committed to memory or spontaneous prayer. Take approximately ten minutes to offer spontaneous vocal prayer to God. Do not rush. Allow an interval of silence after each person has prayed aloud.

Sharing Question

• What was this vocal prayer experience like for you?

Reflection 2

What is the Lord asking?

Meditation consists of seeking "to understand the why and how of the Christian life, in order to adhere and respond to what the Lord is asking" (*CCC*, 2705). There are many aids to beginning meditative prayer—reading the Scriptures, for example, and especially the practice of *lectio divina*, which is explained in this chapter; reading liturgical texts or works on spirituality; focusing on God's works in creation or in the events of history. In meditation, we engage our "thought, imagination, emotion, and desire" (*CCC*, 2708) to explore how the things we have read or seen intersect with our own lives. We journey from the thoughts that arise in us to the reality that we are a part of every day. We listen in order to determine what God wants of us (*CCC*, 2706).

Group meditation

The following format is suggested for you to use as a group for meditative prayer. Take about twenty minutes. Have one person read the following text based on Mark 10:46-52. As the passage is slowly read, stay with the words and images that especially catch your attention. Then imagine the situation, and become aware of the images and feelings awakened in you. End with an expression of your gratitude and love for God.

My name is Joanna. I live in Jericho down near the Jordan River. People have lived there for thousands of years, but I doubt that there has ever been more excitement there than there was this morning. That teacher, Jesus, was in the city, and as he and his friends were leaving a big crowd was following him. Some of the people were trying to listen to what he was saying as he walked along; some of them were asking him questions or arguing with him, or just trying to get his attention. I have heard people call Jesus everything from a messiah to a troublemaker, so I stopped to listen too, but I couldn't get close and the crowd was drowning him out. To make matters worse, Bartimaeus, a blind beggar, started to shout, "Jesus, Son of David, have mercy on me!" Bartimaeus is always annoying people who walk past that spot, and now he was annoying us, because we couldn't hear Jesus as it was. We tried to shut Bartimaeus up, but he just got louder. Finally, Jesus heard him and said, "Call him here." I was a little embarrassed when Jesus looked in our direction, and I pretended I had not been harassing Bartimaeus, but other people told him, "Take heart; get up, he is calling you."

Bartimaeus does not own anything other than that raggedy cloak he always wears, but he threw that off and ran over to Jesus. There was dead silence. Jesus asked Bartimaeus, "What do you want me to do for you?" Bartimaeus said, "My teacher, let me see again." Jesus said to him, "Go. Your faith has made you well." In an instant, Bartimaeus was like a man just let out of prison—jumping up and down, hugging Jesus, and running around touching things that he had never seen before, while we all whooped as if he were a trained monkey. I thought to myself, "How is this possible? Maybe he was never blind to begin with." Jesus watched him for a couple of minutes and then turned to continue on his way. Most people did not notice, but Bartimaeus did. He stopped his celebrating, left his old cloak and us in the dust, and followed Jesus out of the city.

Take a few moments of silence to reflect on the following questions:

- What happened as you were praying? How did you feel? What touched you?
- Why did people want to prevent Bartimaeus from getting Jesus' attention?
- Why did Jesus single out the beggar from all the people gathered there?
- What was the mood of those left behind after Jesus and Bartimaeus had gone?

Reflect on what this passage says to you in your life.

- What person in this passage can you identify with?
- What would you have thought about this incident if you had been in that crowd? Do you ever ask of Jesus things that seem impossible?

Hearing God's voice in Scripture

An ancient form of meditative prayer, practiced privately and in community, is *lectio divina*. This practice reflects our faith that while God speaks to all generations he also speaks to each of us. This method begins with an unhurried reading—a "prayer reading"—of a scripture passage in which the Word can become a place to experience communion with God. We read with awareness that God is present in his Word, and we open what St. Benedict called "the ears of our hearts" to what God's voice may be saying to us beneath and beyond the literal meaning of the verses.

Lectio divina is an occasion to be still in order to hear God's voice as Elijah heard it in the silence that followed wind, earthquake and fire (1 *Kgs:* 19:13). The first movement of this process is *lectio,* reading and listening: we read reverently and attentively as we listen for that word, verse, or passage that resonates with us personally. The next movement is *meditatio:* we reflect on that fragment of scripture. We carefully re-read it, repeat it to ourselves, asking ourselves what God is saying, what prayer, intention or action he is calling us to.

Next we engage in *oratio:* as God's Word emerges from the text, we engage in prayerful dialog with him, accepting the effect of this more intimate understanding of his will on how we live our lives. Then, having listened to God and answered his Word, we engage in contemplation, spending time in silence, contemplating his presence, his message, and his call.

As a group, pray for the power to know God's will and the grace to do his will in your daily life.

Last, offer a prayer of thanks to God for his wondrous deeds.

Living the Good News

Jesus emphasized the connection between faith and action, between what we believe and what we do. In that spirit, decide on an individual or group action that flows from what you have shared in this session. If you decide to act on your own, share your decision with the group. If you decide on a group action, determine among you which individual members will take responsibility for various aspects of the action.

You are likely to benefit most from taking an action that arises from your own response to the session. However, you can consider one of the following suggestions or use these ideas to help develop one of your own:

- Write in your journal about what happed while you meditated on the Scriptures.

- With your pastor and/or parish staff, plan an evening of reflection and meditation, and invite the entire parish.

- In your prayer time this week, bring the marginalized people of the world into God's presence and be in solidarity with them.

- Arrange for someone experienced with *lectio divina* to lead a group in your community.

As my response to the Gospel of Jesus, I commit to:

_____

_____

Lifting Our Hearts

Use your voices to spontaneously thank God for what he has done for you during this session or at any time during this program.

Pray together.

Almighty God,
we thank you for the gift of the Scriptures
through which you speak to us
in words inspired by your Holy Spirit.

As we read and meditate on your word
help us to hear clearly what you are telling us
and how we should apply your message
in our lives.

We ask this through our Lord Jesus Christ,
your son, who lives and reigns with you in the unity
of the Holy Spirit, One God forever and ever.

Amen.

Looking Ahead

- Prepare for your next session by prayerfully reading and studying:
    - Session 8: Contemplative Prayer;
    - Scripture: Lk 15:4-7 (the parable of the lost sheep);
    - *United States Catholic Catechism for Adults,* Chapter 35, "God Calls Us to Pray," p. 474 on "Contemplative Prayer";
    - paragraphs 2709-1719, and paragraph 2724 on contemplative prayer in the *Catechism of the Catholic Church.*
- Remember to use RENEWING FAMILY FAITH and its helpful suggestions on how to extend the fruits of your sharing beyond your group, especially to your families. See page 93.

Contemplative Prayer

Suggested Environment

You may have a Bible—open to the reading for this session—displayed on a small table along with a burning candle. With the Bible, display a picture of Jesus, which will be helpful for the contemplative prayer experience in this session. Soft, reflective music playing in the background might be appropriate for this session. Consider decorating the table with the color of the liturgical season and other symbols of faith.

In addition, it is helpful to have available the Catechism of the Catholic Church (CCC) *and the* United States Catholic Catechism for Adults (USCCA).

Begin with a quiet, reflective atmosphere.

Lifting Our Hearts

Song Suggestion

"You Are Mine," David Haas

Prayer

Pray together.

Ever-present God,
as we gather in this small community,
to share and deepen our faith,
we put other interests and concerns aside.

Still, we are conscious of the pressures,
the distractions and temptations,
that can fill our hours and our days.

We ask you in your Holy Spirit
to give us the clear vision and strength of purpose

to make the time to be alone with you,
our first and dearest Friend.

We ask this through Jesus Christ, our Lord.

Amen.

Sharing Our Good News

Before continuing, take a few moments to share with the group something
of your experience of prayer since our last meeting, including anything that
might have resulted from "Living the Good News."

Reflection 1

"A close sharing between friends"

Elizabeth Catez started out as an "army brat." She was born in a
military camp in France; her father was a captain, and her mother
the daughter of a commandant. Elizabeth was affectionate, but
she qualified for the title of "brat" in a literal way because of her
unwieldy temper. Around the age of seven, affected by the deaths of
her grandfather and father, Elizabeth formed an ambition to become
a nun. Her mother was against it, and the two struggled hard over
the issue for 14 years. Meanwhile, although she loved music, dance,
and fashion, Elizabeth mastered her temperament and developed a
deep spirituality with the Eucharist at its center. Finally, she entered
a Carmelite community in 1901. From an early age, Elizabeth was
aware of the presence of God within her. Not long after she took her
vows, Elizabeth was diagnosed with a disease that was incurable
at that time. As she anticipated death, she said that her mission
in heaven would be to be to help people find God in silence and
simplicity. Elizabeth died at twenty-six in 1906 and was beatified
Blessed Elizabeth of the Trinity by Pope John Paul II in 1984.

Sharing Question

• Briefly summarize your spiritual "biography"—your journey to
  an adult relationship with God from early childhood through your
  years as a teenager and a young adult.

Contemplative prayer, according to St. Teresa of Ávila, "is nothing
else than a close sharing between friends; it means taking time
frequently to be alone with him who we know loves us" (St. Teresa
of Jesus, The Book of Her Life, 8, 5 in *The collected works of St. Teresa of*

Avila, tr. K. Kavanaugh, OCD, and O. Rodriguez, OCD [Washington, DC: Institute of Carmelite Studies, 1976], I, 67) (*CCC*, 2709). Often, when we are alone with a friend, words are unnecessary. Unlike vocal prayer or active meditation, contemplative prayer is a quiet state— the silence and simplicity urged by Blessed Elizabeth—in which our minds and imaginations are at rest, and we focus on God's presence. In her "Prayer to the Holy Trinity," Elizabeth asked God, "help me forget myself entirely so to establish myself in you, unmovable and peaceful as if my soul were already in eternity" (Prayer of Blessed Elizabeth of the Trinity) (*CCC*, 260).

"One does not undertake contemplative prayer only when one has the time: one makes time for the Lord, with the firm determination not to give up, no matter what trials and dryness one may encounter. One cannot always meditate, but one can always enter into inner prayer, independently of the conditions of health, work, or emotional state" (*CCC*, 2710).

Contemplation is a great act of love. We desire God as God desires us. We give our hearts to God, and it is within our hearts that we encounter God in his Son through the promptings of the Holy Spirit. We recall again that the great mystery is not our love for God, but God's total and unconditional love for us—the God who seeks us, not in some impersonal manner, but with true intimacy. In the Gospel of Luke, we hear Jesus use a parable to express the love God has for us in the image of a lamb nestled safely on the shepherd's shoulders:

Pondering the Word

Love begins with God

Luke 15:4-7

Sharing Questions

- Take a moment to reflect on what word, phrase, or image from the scripture passage touches your heart or speaks to your life. Reflect in silence on your thoughts, or share them aloud.

- Recall a time when have you felt that God had in some way rescued you or someone you know.

Making the heart a place for prayer

"It is not necessary for being with God to be always at church; we may make an oratory of our heart, wherein to retire from time to time, to converse with Him in meekness, humility, and love. Every one is capable of such familiar conversation with God, some more, some less: He knows what we can do."

Brother Lawrence, 17th-century Discalced Carmelite

Reflection 2

Gazing at the Lord

Contemplative prayer is, in a sense, "a gaze of faith, fixed on Jesus" (*CCC*, 2715). A peasant who used to sit before the tabernacle in the church at Ars while St. John Vianney was ministering there described in simple terms what took place between him and the Lord: "I look at him, and he looks at me" (*CCC*, 2715). In contemplation, a person puts aside the self—the "me"—and sees everything only in terms of the Gospel and the unconditional compassion of Jesus Christ.

Contemplative prayer requires few if any words, a model we are not used to in everyday life. "Words in this kind of prayer are not speeches; they are like kindling that feeds the fire of love" (*CCC*, 2717). "Like all good prayer, this form requires a regular time each day. When one gives God time for prayer, he will give time for one's other responsibilities" (*USCCA*, p. 474).

Contemplative prayer

Take twenty minutes for contemplative prayer together. Place the picture of Jesus in a place where it can easily be seen by every member of the group. During this contemplative prayer, instrumental spiritual music, preferably not widely familiar so that it does not distract the group, may be playing in the background.

- Settle into a comfortable position, taking slow, deep breaths to help quiet yourself.

- Focus your attention on the image of Jesus.

- Acknowledge the things that are trying to get your attention— thoughts, worries, plans, aches and pains, sights and sounds around you. Slowly let these things go. If you feel distracted during this prayer, just quietly bring yourself back to your reflection.

- In your silence and stillness, let God's Spirit within you make itself known.

- Do not expect anything to "happen"; put yourself in God's hands.

When the group leader indicates that the time of prayers is ending by softly beginning to pray the Lord's Prayer, join in the prayer, letting yourself emerge gradually from your quiet state.

Sharing Questions

- What was the experience of contemplative prayer like for you?

- If you don't usually pray like this, how can you rearrange relationships or activities in your life in order to have the necessary time and the quiet?

Living the Good News

Jesus emphasized the connection between faith and action, between what we believe and what we do. In that spirit, decide on an individual or group action that flows from what you have shared in this session. If you decide to act on your own, share your decision with the group. If you decide on a group action, determine among you which individual members will take responsibility for various aspects of the action.

"With sighs too deep for words"

"We know that the whole creation has been groaning in labor pains until now; and not only the creation, but we ourselves, who have the first fruits of the Spirit, groan inwardly while we wait for adoption, the redemption of our bodies. For in hope we were saved. Now hope that is seen is not hope. For who hopes for what is seen? But if we hope for what we do not see, we wait for it with patience. Likewise the Spirit helps us in our weakness; for we do not know how to pray as we ought, but that very Spirit intercedes with sighs too deep for words. And God, who searches the heart, knows what is the mind of the Spirit, because the Spirit intercedes for the saints according to the will of God."

Rom 8:22-27

You are likely to benefit most from taking an action that arises from your own response to the session. However, you can consider one of the following suggestions or use these ideas to help develop one of your own:

- Commit yourself to 15 minutes of contemplative prayer at least once a week.

- Join with others in contemplative prayer.

- Read and study:
    - *Catechism of the Catholic Church,* paragraphs 2709-2719 and paragraph 2724 on contemplative prayer;
    - *United States Catholic Catechism for Adults,* Chapter 35, "God Calls Us to Pray," p. 474 on contemplative prayer.

As my response to the Gospel of Jesus, I commit to:

_____

_____

Lifting Our Hearts

Pray together

Almighty God,
Saint Teresa said contemplative prayer
is a conversation between friends.

As we go about our work and play
Help us every day to spend time with you,
	our Friend,
where Blessed Elizabeth found you,
in the depths of our hearts.

We ask this through Jesus Christ, our Lord.

Amen.

Looking Ahead

- Prepare for your next session by prayerfully reading and studying:
  - Session 9: Difficulties in Prayer;
  - Scripture: Matthew 6:24-34 (relying on God for our needs);
  - *United States Catholic Catechism for Adults,* Chapter 35, "God Calls Us to Pray," pp. 476-477;
  - paragraphs 2725-2745 on "The Battle of Prayer" in the *Catechism of the Catholic Church.*
- Remember to use RENEWING FAMILY FAITH and its helpful suggestions on how to extend the fruits of your sharing beyond your group, especially to your families. See page 93.

Difficulties in Prayer

Suggested Environment

You may have a Bible—open to the reading for this session—displayed on a small table along with a burning candle. Consider decorating the table with the color of the liturgical season and other symbols of faith. You may also arrange, in the space where the group meets, some bean seeds, soil, and a small plant container. At the closing prayer, plant the seeds, water them, and leave them in place where the group can watch them grow during the next three sessions.

In addition, it is helpful to have available the Catechism of the Catholic Church (CCC) *and the* United States Catholic Catechism for Adults (USCCA).

Begin with a quiet, reflective atmosphere.

Lifting Our Hearts

Song Suggestion

"Holy Darkness," Dan Schutte

Prayer

Pray together

Ever-present God,
as we come together in this faith community
we ask you in your Holy Spirit to give us the wisdom
to clearly understand our relationship with you in prayer.

Help us, dear God, to pray without hesitating,
to pray with persistence,
to pray with humility,
and to pray without being discouraged,
remembering that we can do nothing without you
and that you know and want for us
only those things that will draw us closer to you.

We ask this through Jesus Christ, our Lord.

Amen.

Sharing Our Good News

Before continuing, take a few moments to share with the group something of your experience of prayer since our last meeting, including anything that may have resulted from "Living the Good News."

Reflection 1

Fighting the "battle" of prayer

St. Scholastica and St. Benedict were twins who lived in Italy in the fifth and sixth centuries. When they entered religious life, their communities were both in the area of Monte Cassino. Once a year, Scholastica would visit Benedict at a spot outside the gate of his monastery. During one of these visits—only three days before her death—Scholastica spent the whole day talking with Benedict and some of his brother monks about sacred subjects. When they had eaten supper together and it was getting late, Scholastica tried to convince Benedict to spend the whole night talking to her, but he insisted he had to return to his monastic cell. When Scholastica couldn't convince him, she folded her hands on the table, put her head down on them and began to pray. As she finished, a violent storm came up with lightning, thunder, and torrential rain. "What have you done?" Benedict asked his sister. "Well," she said, "I asked you, and you wouldn't listen; so I asked God, and he did listen. So now, go off, if you can, and return to your monastery." Benedict sat up with his sister all night.

Sharing Question

• Are you more likely to turn to God as a first resort or as a last resort?

Prayer is not always easy. While the opportunity to pray is a gift from God, prayer requires an effort on our part. Making that effort can bring us face to face with challenges that include the idiosyncrasies of human life, the habit of sin, and the need to keep growing in spirituality.

Prayer can be difficult because the attitudes and atmosphere in our society work against it. Some people prize production and profit above all things and think only in terms of the present world, so prayer may seem useless to them. "Still others exalt sensuality and comfort as the criteria of the true, the good, and the beautiful; whereas prayer, the 'love of beauty' ... is caught up in the glory of the living and true God" (*CCC*, 2727). The constant noise in our culture and the seemingly insatiable appetite for it may make reflection and quiet feel unfamiliar and uncomfortable. Excessive materialism may lead many to consider prayer an escape from reality, a practice that does not make sense in a world of reason and science.

A common problem in prayer is distraction—the intrusion of unrelated thoughts or images that take our attention away from our encounter with God. The *Catechism* points out the importance of such a moment. Which is more important to us, the distraction itself—the dinner reservation, the football pool, the book club meeting—or our determination to put it aside and turn our hearts back to God? And so, "a distraction reveals to us what we are attached to." "Therein lies the battle," the *Catechism* tells us, "the choice of which master to serve" (Cf. *Mt* 6:21, 24) (*CCC*, 2729).

Our prayer life can be disrupted also by a lack of faith. This can mean that we do not wholly trust in God's promise to hear and answer our prayers. It can mean that we presume on God's generosity before we have fully given over our hearts to him. Or it can mean that we have not accepted our total dependence on God and believe in our own power more than in his. We frequently make our prayer through Jesus, but have we turned to him with unconditional humility and trust? Do we believe what he has told us: "Apart from me you can do nothing"? (*Jn* 15:5) (*CCC*, 2092, 2732)

We can see from this discussion that prayer puts us to the test, and nowhere more than in our prayers of petition—prayers in which we seek help for others or for ourselves. Indeed, some stop praying if they think that God has not heard them (*CCC*, 2734). On this point, the *Catechism* poses a question: when we

Spotlight on the *Catechism*

"It is often said that we should pray as if everything depended on God and act as if everything depended on us. The 'can-do' mindset of our culture inclines many believers to substitute self-reliance for prayer. People are not conscious of their need for God.

Despite the general cultural preference for an independent spirit that idealizes the achievements of the self in getting things done, studies about religion indicate a significant counter movement. Virtually all Americans claim they believe in God. A high number of people report they pray each day."

United States Catholic Catechism for Adults, p. 476

demand results from our prayers, what image of God do we have in our minds—an "instrument" that we can use to get what we want, or our creator and redeemer? (*CCC*, 2735) God knows what we need—not just what we want—before we ask him (Cf. *Mt* 6:8). We pray in order to discover what God wants (Cf. *Rom* 8:27) (*CCC*, 2735-2736).

Sharing Question

• Recall a time when God's will, rather than your own, became clear to you in prayer.

Pondering the Word

"Strive first for the kingdom of God"

As Christians, we are called to face the difficulties of prayer with humility, with trust in God, and with perseverance. One step toward improving our prayer life is examining our priorities, as Jesus explains so clearly in this gospel passage:

Matthew 6:24-34

Sharing Questions

• Take a moment to reflect on what word, phrase, or image from the scripture passage touches your heart or speaks to your life. Reflect in silence on your thoughts, or share them aloud.

• What have been your personal struggles with prayer? How do the words of Jesus in the gospel passage help you in that struggle?

Reflection 2

"He heard when I cried to him"

We began these sessions by reflecting on the idea that prayer is the love relationship between God and us. That relationship is disrupted by sin—which in itself is self-indulgence, a turn inward and away from God. Habitual sin—whether it takes the form of injustice, adultery, pornography, or abuse of alcohol or drugs—distorts the relationship to the point that prayer, a love relationship with God, becomes impossible. But God doesn't turn away. God is always present, always looking our way, always waiting for us to acknowledge our sin, face him squarely again, and ask for his unfailing mercy and help.

The *Catechism* article that discusses the topics of this session is entitled "The Battle of Prayer" (*CCC*, pp 653-658). Because prayer is at times a serene experience, "battle" may seem at first like an odd metaphor. But that word expresses the fact that prayer life is dynamic. As we have already discussed, prayer is a relationship between God and us—a relationship that begins with God's call. Relationships are give-and-take affairs that have their ups and downs, their misunderstandings, their moments of intensity and their dry spells. Still, if both parties to a relationship are persistent in their love of each other, the relationship develops and deepens over time. So it is with prayer.

It is not unusual for those who are faithful to prayer to feel at times that God isn't "listening," that God isn't "answering," that they are not "getting anything" out of prayer, or that doubts about their faith make prayer seem futile. Those feelings may arise because God is calling them into a deeper experience. When we have been faithful to prayer, the discomfort we experience, or the sense of being unable to pray, is an invitation from God to let him lead us. Our "work" is to show up and pay attention. Gradually, we learn to follow God's lead into deeper prayer.

Murky periods in their prayer lives have been described, for example, by St. Teresa of Ávila, St. Thérèse of Lisieux, St. John of the Cross, St. Paul of the Cross, and Mother Teresa of Calcutta. The sensation of a "dead end" in prayer is also mentioned in the Psalms, including the familiar Psalm 22, "My God, my God, why have you forsaken me?

"Time devoted to prayer is not time wasted"

"In our society, which all too often lacks spiritual values, St Teresa (of Ávila) teaches us to be unflagging witnesses of God, of his presence and of his action. She teaches us truly to feel this thirst for God that exists in the depths of our hearts, this desire to see God, to seek God, to be in conversation with him and to be his friends.

This is the friendship we all need that we must seek anew, day after day. May the example of this Saint … spur us too every day to dedicate the right time to prayer, to this openness to God, to this journey, in order to seek God, to see him, to discover his friendship and so to find true life. …

Therefore time devoted to prayer is not time wasted, it is time in which the path of life unfolds, the path unfolds to learning from God an ardent love for him, for his Church, and practical charity for our brothers and sisters."

Pope Benedict XVI, *General Audience*, February 2, 2011

Why are you so far from helping me, from the words of my groaning? O my God, I cry by day, but you do not answer; and by night, but find no rest" (*Ps* 22:1-3). But the Psalmist was persistent, acknowledging despite the difficulties of life that he owed life itself to God, and ultimately expressing his faith in God's kindness: "You who fear the Lord, praise him! All you offspring of Jacob, glorify him; stand in awe of him, all you offspring of Israel! For he did not despise or abhor the affliction of the afflicted; he did not hide his face from me, but heard when I cried to him" (*Ps* 22:23-24).

Getting through such times in our prayer lives involves, first of all, keeping at it—not giving up. But because prayer is a vital relationship, we may deepen it precisely by looking at it more deeply: honestly considering the distractions and assumptions we have discussed in this session, but also increasing our awareness of the spiritual life through reading, such as the suggestions made in the Reflection in Session One, or seeking a spiritual director, as we discussed in Session Six.

Our challenge is to persevere in love and to "pray without ceasing" (1 *Thes* 5:17). St. Paul meant that literally. No matter where we are, we can pray. We can pray while we walk, while we ride the bus or train, while we do our jobs, while we pause at work and glance out a window, while we cook or clean at home. By praying constantly, we recognize that our time belongs to God. Our prayer also expresses our faith in the promise Jesus made: "I am with you always" (*Mt* 28:20).

Sharing Questions

- Do you sometimes feel that prayer is useless? If so, how do you deal with that feeling? If not, why are you confident?

- What moments in your daily life—trips to and from work, coffee breaks, lunch breaks, housework, yard work—could be new occasions for prayer for you?

Living the Good News

Jesus emphasized the connection between faith and action, between what we believe and what we do. In that spirit, decide on an individual or group action that flows from what you have shared in this session. If you decide to act on your own, share your decision with the group. If you decide on a group action, determine among you which individual members will take responsibility for various aspects of the action.

*You are likely to benefit most from taking an action that arises from your
own response to the session. However, you can consider one of the following
suggestions or use these ideas to help develop one of your own:*

- When distractions arise as you pray, make a conscious effort to
  gently turn your heart back to God.
- Pray for the needs of others.
- Use your prayer journal to express your experiences in prayer.

As my response to the Gospel of Jesus, I commit to:

_____

_____

Lifting Our Hearts

*Take a few minutes to reflect on obstacles that keep you from prayer or
interrupt your prayer. Spontaneously pray for God to help you avoid or
overcome these obstacles.*

*Pray together in alternating groups or in groups of participants on opposite
sides of the room:*

Group 1	O Lord, Jesus Christ, you who said,
Group 2	"I tell you solemnly, if anyone says to this mountain, 'Get up and throw yourself into the sea,' with no hesitation in his or her heart, believing that it will happen, it will be done,"
Group 1	increase our faith this day. Let it grow at least to the size of a mustard seed. Help us, O Lord, to believe impossible things and to trust you with our hearts and not just our heads.
All	**We ask this of you who live and reign with God our Father and the Holy Spirit forever and ever. Amen.**

Adapted from *Let's Pray* by Charles Reutemann, FSC

Looking Ahead

- Prepare for your next session by prayerfully reading and studying:
  - Session 10: As Jesus Taught Us: The Lord's Prayer;
  - Scripture: Matthew 6:7-13 (The Lord's Prayer);
  - *United States Catholic Catechism for Adults,* Chapter 36 "Jesus Taught Us to Pray," pp. 481-483 on Matthew's and Luke's versions of the Lord's Prayer, and pp. 484-485 on "We Address the Father";
  - paragraphs 2759-2785 of the *Catechism of the Catholic Church.*
- Remember to use RENEWING FAMILY FAITH and its helpful suggestions on how to extend the fruits of your sharing beyond your group, especially to your families. See page 93.

As Jesus Taught Us:
The Lord's Prayer

Suggested Environment

You may have a Bible—open to either Matthew 6:9-13 or Luke 11:1-4 —displayed on a small table along with a burning candle. For the next three sessions, you may also display the Lord's Prayer, in large print, near the Bible. Consider decorating the table with colors of the liturgical season and other symbols of faith.

In addition, it is helpful to have available the Catechism of the Catholic Church (CCC) *and the* United States Catholic Catechism for Adults (USCCA).

Begin with a quiet, reflective atmosphere.

Lifting Our Hearts

Song Suggestion

"The Lord's Prayer," music by Steven C. Warner

Prayer

Almighty God,
we come together as a people
to reflect on the prayer we have received
from your divine Son.

Help us, dear God, to hear this prayer with fresh ears
pray it with fresh lips
and ponder it with fresh minds.

Help us to live in its spirit
by worshipping and praising you,
by relying only on you,
by repenting our sins,
by forgiving those who have wronged us,
and by seeking you before all things.

We ask this through Jesus Christ, our Lord.

Amen.

Sharing Our Good News

Before continuing, take a few moments to share with the group something of your experience of prayer since our last meeting, including anything that might have resulted from "Living the Good News."

Reflection 1

"Teach us to pray"

The Lord's Prayer is part of the worship of Christians in almost every denomination. The prayer is so well known that it was set to music in 1935 by Albert Hay Malotte, a composer, musician, and teacher who wrote more than 200 songs, many of them for movie scores, including the music for Walt Disney's "Ferdinand the Bull" and "The Ugly Duckling." Malotte's best known work by far, however, was his musical setting for the Lord's Prayer, which has been performed by professional singers and sung by choirs and congregations for more than seven decades. One indication of the broad appeal of this version of the prayer is the variety of singers who have recorded it. Among others, they include Sarah Vaughn, Kate Smith, Mahalia Jackson, Doris Day, Patti Page, Nelson Eddy, Johnny Mathis, Frank Sinatra, Perry Como, Elvis Presley, Boots Randolph, Ronnie Milsap, José Carreras, Andrea Bocelli, the Statler Brothers, the Beach Boys, Il Divo, Richard Tucker, and Barbra Streisand.

Sharing Question

• The Lord's Prayer has an almost universal appeal that surpasses that of any other individual Christian prayer. In what way is this prayer special for you?

After Jesus' disciples had seen him so often at prayer, one of them said, "Lord, teach us to pray" (*Lk* 11:1). Jesus responded by giving his disciples—both then and through the ages—a prayer so fundamental that the third century Christian writer Tertullian called it "the summary of the whole gospel (Tertullian, *De oratione* 1:PL 1, 1155)" (*CCC*, 2761). St. Luke's gospel presents the prayer with five petitions (*Lk* 11:2-4), and St. Matthew's gospel presents a fuller version with seven petitions (*Mt* 6:9-13). It is from St. Matthew's text that the

Church has derived The Lord's Prayer (*CCC*, 2759). Our final three sessions will be devoted to reflections on this gift from our Lord. You are invited to consider not only what the prayer says—"the words our Savior gave us"—but also what a model it is for all of our prayer, in which we acknowledge and praise God, submit our will to his, and ask him for those things that are truly good for us. You are invited to listen to this familiar prayer with new ears and open hearts.

Pondering the Word

"Pray in this way"

Matthew 6:7-13

Read each verse and then pause for a few minutes, allowing the members of the group to reflect.

Sharing Question

• What words of Jesus particularly touched you as you listened again to the Lord's Prayer read from Scripture?

Reflection 2

The prayer and the Spirit

Spotlight on the *Catechism*

"The Our Father is called the 'Lord's Prayer' because Jesus, our Lord and model of prayer, is its author.…

St. Augustine wrote seven commentaries on the Our Father. So moved was he by its depth that he wrote, 'Run through all the words of holy prayers [in Scripture], and I do not think you will find anything in them that is not contained in the Lord's Prayer' (*Letter*, 130, 12, 22) …. It is at the heart of every individual and communal prayer."

United States Catholic Catechism for Adults, p. 483

Jesus gave us this prayer during the Sermon on the Mount. In that sermon, specifically in the Beatitudes, he set the tone for his own ministry—embracing the poor, the merciful, and the marginalized. He also told his followers how to live: keep the commandments; put aside anger; don't hold grudges; avoid occasions of sin; be faithful to vows; don't seek revenge for injuries; help those who ask; love those who harm you (*Mt* 5:21-48). Jesus—in whom the Law, the Prophets, and the Psalms had been fulfilled—was asking more of his disciples than had been demanded of them by the faith of their ancestors. It was in the midst of teaching this new life that he gave us the prayer in which we ask God to help us live that very life (*CCC*, 2763-2764).

In giving us this prayer, however, Jesus does not give us a formula to repeat as though it were a charm or a mantra. He gives us the

Spotlight on the *Catechism*

"When we say 'Our', we recognize that we are a people bound together by the New Covenant that God has made with us through his Son in the Holy Spirit. While we are indeed individual persons, we are also persons in communion with each other because we have been baptized into communion with the Holy Trinity. The Our Father is a prayer of the Church, hence we pray with the Church when we recite these words, together calling God our Father."

United States Catholic Catechism for Adults, p. 485

words, but he also gives us the Spirit through whom these words enliven us. Whenever we pray with these words, we are responding to the Spirit by expressing our faith in our Creator, and we are committing ourselves once again to submit our will to his will (*CCC*, 2766).

The Lord's Prayer has been at the center of the Church's worship from the beginning. In fact, the *Didache*—a catechism dating from the late first or early second century—includes the text of the Lord's Prayer and directs Christians to pray it three times a day (*CCC*, 2767). The Lord's Prayer is a component of *The Liturgy of the Hours* or Divine Office and the celebration of the sacraments of Baptism, Confirmation, and Eucharist. In the Eucharistic celebration, the Lord's Prayer is offered as the "prayer of the whole Church" (*CCC*, 2767-2771). "At Mass, it comes after the Eucharistic Prayer, summing up the intercessions of that prayer and preparing us for Holy Communion when we receive Jesus Christ, who is the Bread of Life" (*USCCA*, p. 483).

In the third edition of the *Roman Missal,* the celebrant invites us to pray the Lord's Prayer with the phrase "we dare to say." This phrase reminds us that it is only through Jesus and in the Holy Spirit that we can speak to God in this way. It is Jesus who reveals God to us as Trinity, and so it is Jesus who reveals to us that we can speak to God as our "Father." We cannot comprehend the relationship among the Persons of the Trinity, and yet through Jesus we can participate in that relationship by receiving and returning God's love with the simplicity of children and by behaving as his sons and daughters (*CCC*, 2777, 2779-2780, 2784-2785).

Sharing Questions

• Which part of the Lord's Prayer challenges you? Which part comforts you?

• How do you see the Lord's Prayer as a model for living?

- How can you keep aware of the meaning of a familiar prayer such as the Lord's Prayer?

Living the Good News

Jesus emphasized the connection between faith and action, between what we believe and what we do. In that spirit, decide on an individual or group action that flows from what you have shared in this session. If you decide to act on your own, share your decision with the group. If you decide on a group action, determine among you which individual members will take responsibility for various aspects of the action.

You are likely to benefit most from taking an action that arises from your own response to the session. However, you can consider one of the following suggestions or use these ideas to help develop one of your own:

- If you are a parent, choose an action to show greater love to your child. If your own parents are living, choose an action to show them your love.
- Pray for someone who has offended you. Forgive that person.
- Reach out to children who are in need of love.
- Pray the Lord's Prayer three times a day.

As my response to the Gospel of Jesus, I commit to:

_____

_____

Lifting Our Hearts

Take about ten minutes for a silent meditation. Settle into a comfortable position. Take slow, deep breaths. Let go of things that might distract you—sounds and sights in this room, worries and obligations that are on your mind.

Reflect on the ways God has been a loving parent to you or those close to you.

(Sit in silent meditation until your leader resumes the session.)

Offer vocal prayers of thanks to God for what he has done as Parent for you or others.

Pray together.

Almighty God,
you created us,
you made us in your own image
you gave us charge over the earth
and all that it contains.

We who are your children
thank you for all these things
through Jesus Christ our Lord.

Amen.

Offer each other a sign of God's peace.

Looking Ahead

- Prepare for your next session by prayerfully reading and studying:
    - Session 11: We Glorify God: The Lord's Prayer;
    - Scripture: Matthew 5:21-26 (loving our enemies, forgiving wrongs);
- You may like to consult the relevant paragraphs from the *Catechism of the Catholic Church:*
    - paragraphs 2786-2793 on "Our Father"
    - paragraphs 2794-2796 on "Who Art in Heaven"
    - paragraphs 2803-2806 introducing the seven petitions
    - paragraphs 2807-2815 on "Hallowed Be Thy Name"
    - paragraphs 2816-2821 on "Thy Kingdom Come"
    - paragraphs 2822-2827 on "Thy Will Be Done on Earth"
- You might also want to read the *United States Catholic Catechism for Adults,* Chapter 36 "Jesus Taught Us to Pray," pp. 485-487 on the first four petitions in the Lord's Prayer.
- Remember to use RENEWING FAMILY FAITH and its helpful suggestions on how to extend the fruits of your sharing beyond your group, especially to your families. See page 93.

We Glorify God:
The Lord's Prayer

Suggested Environment

You may have a Bible—open to the reading for this session—displayed on a small table along with a burning candle. For the next two sessions, you may display with the Bible newspaper or magazine articles that deal with the theme of reconciliation. Consider decorating the table with the color of the liturgical season and other symbols of faith.

In addition, it is helpful to have available the Catechism of the Catholic Church (CCC) *and the* United States Catholic Catechism for Adults (USCCA).

Begin with a quiet, reflective atmosphere.

Lifting Our Hearts

Song Suggestion

"Sing a New Church," Sr. Delores Dufner, OSB

Prayer

Ever-present God,
as we gather to reflect on our faith,
we "raise" our hearts and voices to heaven
in praise and thanks to you.

Still, we know that you are not in some far-off place
but here with us when we gather in your name
and even closer, in the heart of every one who loves you.

Help us, dear God, to be ever more conscious that you are near
and that neither space nor time can come between us
when we call on you in prayer.

We ask this through our Lord, Jesus Christ.

Amen.

Sharing Our Good News

Before continuing, take a few moments to share with the group something of your experience of prayer since our last meeting, including anything that might have resulted from "Living the Good News."

Reflection 1

"Our Father"

In the liturgical calendar, we find the names of many individual saints. Some of the names may be familiar—St. Elizabeth Ann Seton on January 4, St. Anthony of Padua on June 13, St. Clare on August 11, St. Francis of Assisi on October 4. Others may seem obscure to many of us—St. Theophilus of Corte on May 19, St. Jeanne Jugan on August 30, St. Gertrude on November 16. And some saints—members of groups of Catholics who shared similar experiences—are not named at all on the calendar because there were so many of them. These include the unnamed Korean Martyrs, commemorated on September 20 along with Saints Andrew Kim Taegôn and Paul Chông Hasang, and the unnamed Vietnamese Martyrs commemorated on November 24 along with St. Andrew Dung-Lac. All of these were victims of religious persecution: at least 8,000 in Korea in the 19th century, and an unknown figure—perhaps hundreds of thousands—in Vietnam from the 17th to the 19th centuries. They died in circumstances and in places that are far from the experience of most Catholics, and yet they professed the same faith and shared in the same Eucharist that we do. They are part of the "our" in "Our Father."

Sharing Question

- How conscious are you of who is included when you pray, "our Father," "give us," "forgive us," "lead us not," and "deliver us"?

The "our" in "Our Father" does not suggest that we possess God but rather that we have entered into a new relationship with him. When we say "our Father," we are recognizing what the death and resurrection of Jesus has made possible: we have become "his" people and he is forever "our" God (CCC, 2786-2787). Although we pray to the Father in the words the Son gave us, we are not dividing the Holy Trinity. "When we pray to the Father, we adore and glorify him together with the Son and the Holy Spirit" (CCC, 2789). When we say "our" Father, we also express the fact that we are a family—

the Church—who are united with God in this new relationship (*CCC*, 2790). We cannot pray the Lord's Prayer without recognizing that we live in a society with a strong emphasis on individualism and that we are called to leave that individualism behind and work to overcome any divisions among us so that we exclude no one from our prayer and love all people unconditionally (*CCC*, 2792-2793).

Sharing Question

• How would your sense of the Church be affected if you consciously said "we" more often than "I" in your personal prayer?

Pondering the Word

"First be reconciled"

Matthew 5:21-26

Sharing Questions

• Take a moment to reflect on what word, phrase, or image from the scripture passage touches your heart or speaks to your life. Reflect in silence on your thoughts, or share them aloud.

• Jesus asks us to unconditionally forgive others who have wronged us. Whom do you feel the need to forgive?

Reflection 2

"Who Art in Heaven"

Our prayer, "Our Father who art in heaven," does not mean that God is confined to a particular place. "Heaven" refers instead to a way of being. God transcends concepts such as space and time that concern us in everyday life. At the same time, far from being distant, God is as present in the hearts of every person who loves him as he is present in the skies (*CCC*, 2794). The symbol of heaven that we refer to in prayer reminds us that we have been "separated" from God by sin and that he wants us to "return" to him through the conversion of our hearts. For that reason, God came "down from heaven" and lived among us in the person of Jesus. Through the death, resurrection, and ascension of Jesus, we, too, can "ascend" to heaven, and we can begin that journey here and now in communion with God and each other in the Church (*CCC*, 2795-2796).

The Seven Petitions

After we have called on God and acknowledged our loving relationship with him, we present to him seven petitions. In the first three, we glorify him; in the last four, we recognize our need for God's grace (*CCC*, 2803).

In a sincere love relationship, we think first of the one we love, and so it is in our relationship with God. In the first three petitions of the Lord's Prayer, we speak to God of "your name," "your kingdom," and "your will," and we do not mention ourselves (*CCC*, 2804). In the last four petitions, we pray "give us," "forgive us," "lead us not," "deliver us," asking God to do what he thinks best for us both at this moment and in eternity (*CCC*, 2805). Notice, though, that these prayers are not for "me" alone but for "us"—for the whole world (*CCC*, 2806).

"Hallowed be thy name"

Most of us use "hallow" as a noun only when we mention Halloween, and most of us use it as a verb only when we are saying the Lord's Prayer. To hallow means to make holy, but the prayer does not mean that *we* make God's name holy. "God is the source of his own holiness that is his perfection and glory. But we give witness to his holiness by doing his will, being people of prayer, and establishing the earthly conditions by which his holiness is manifested" (*USCCA*, pp. 485-486). There is a parallel to this in our own lives. We all have personal names that identify us as unique individuals, and we all try to protect our "good names" among our friends and in the community. Whatever our names are, we can't make them good or bad except by how other people see us living. St. Peter Chrysologus, a fifth-century bishop known for his brief, clear sermons, explained that "we ask that this name of God should be hallowed in us through our actions. For God's name is blessed when we live well, but is blasphemed when

Spotlight on the *Catechism*

"God gradually revealed his name. First of all he revealed it to Moses, through whom he tells us that he is 'I Am', a person who chooses to be close to us yet remains mysterious. As salvation history unfolded, the people of Israel developed other names they used to refer to God, such as Lord, Shepherd of Israel, and King.

But God's definitive revelation of who he is was through Jesus Christ, who taught us that God is his Father and he is the Son. Through Christ's salvation and the Sacrament of Baptism, we become adopted children of God by grace. Hence we can legitimately call God 'Father' "

United States Catholic Catechism for Adults, p. 486

we live wickedly" (*Sermo* 71, 4: PL
52:402A; cf. *Rom* 2:24; *Ezek* 36:20-22)
(*CCC*, 2814).

"Thy kingdom come"

The term "kingdom" is understood
in our Christian faith as both
something to be hoped for and
something to experience now.
When we say, in the Lord's
Prayer," thy kingdom come,"
we are looking forward to Jesus'
promise of the final establishment
of the Reign of God: "I will come
again and will take you to myself,
so that where I am, there you may
be also" (*Jn* 14:3). At the same time,
we recognize that the kingdom is
already in progress. Jesus and John

All that must be said is in this prayer

"When the disciples asked the Lord Jesus, 'Teach us to pray,' He replied by saying the words of the 'Our Father,' thereby giving a concrete model which is also a universal model. In fact, everything that can and must be said to the Father is contained in those seven requests which we all know by heart. There is such simplicity in them that even a child can learn them, but at the same time such depth that a whole life can be spent meditating on their meaning."

John Paul II, *General Audience*, March 14, 1979.

the Baptist proclaimed it; it was fulfilled in the death and resurrection
of Jesus and is present in our midst in the Eucharist (*CCC*, 2816).
Since Pentecost, the coming of the kingdom in this world—torn as it
is between holiness and materialism—has been the work of the Holy
Spirit. Filled with that Spirit, the Church prays for the coming of
God's kingdom in glory, but remains committed to mercy, love, and
justice in this world (*CCC*, 2818-2819). The Church's commitment is
our commitment. The *Catechism* tells us that our aspiration to eternal
life does not suppress but actually reinforces our duty to work for
peace and justice in *this* world (*CCC*, 2820).

"Thy will be done on earth as it is in heaven"

Jesus taught us that all the words in the world, by themselves,
cannot lead us to union with God: "Not everyone who says to me,
'Lord, Lord,' will enter the kingdom of heaven, but only one who
does the will of my Father in heaven" (*Mt* 7:21). Jesus himself, as he
did in all things, provided the perfect example when he prayed on
the Mount of Olives, anticipating imminent suffering and death
(*CCC*, 2824). "Father, if you are willing, remove this cup from me; yet,
not my will but yours be done" (*Lk* 22:42; cf. *Jn* 4:34; 5:30; 6:38). "Not
my will, but yours be done"—that is our prayer in this petition. The
commandment Jesus taught—"Just as I have loved you, you should

also love one another" (*Jn* 13:34; cf. 1 *Jn* 3; 4; *Lk* 10:25-37)—expresses the "entire will" of God" (*CCC*, 2822). Still, in specific situations in our lives, we may find it difficult to know how God wants us to apply this commandment. And even if we do have a sense of God's will, we may find it difficult at times to give up our own. The *Catechism* reminds us, in fact, that while we cannot do it on our own, we can wholly embrace the will of God when we are united with Christ in the Holy Spirit (*CCC*, 2825).

Sharing Questions

• When in your life have you been especially aware of the reign of God as something we experience now?

• What help or spiritual support do you need to better live the prayer "Thy will be done"?

Prayer is the practice of love.

It can change the world.

It sounds so simple, but it is true.

Hold on to hope and find peace in your heart.

Put your trust in God.

Immaculee Ilibagiza, survivor of the Rwanda massacres of 1994. Address at Caldwell College, April 18, 2007.

Living the Good News

Jesus emphasized the connection between faith and action, between what we believe and what we do. In that spirit, decide on an individual or group action that flows from what you have shared in this session. If you decide to act on your own, share your decision with the group. If you decide on a group action, determine among you which individual members will take responsibility for various aspects of the action.

You are likely to benefit most from taking an action that arises from your own response to the session. However, you can consider one of the following suggestions or use these ideas to help develop one of your own:

• Look up the meaning of your name. Thank God for the unique gift of life that is yours.

• Speak with a spiritual friend or guide who can help you reflect on God's will in your life in a particular situation.

• Participate in a local situation, such as a political campaign, that will help bring about greater peace, justice, and harmony in the world.

As my response to the Gospel of Jesus, I commit to:

_____

_____

Lifting Our Hearts

Now let's listen to the Lord's Prayer. During the song and for a few moments afterward, reflect on how these petitions apply to your life: "hallowed be your name," "your kingdom come," "your will be done on earth as it is in heaven." Offer spontaneous prayers prompted by these petitions.

"The Lord's Prayer," traditional chant adapted by Robert J. Snow
Performed by OCP Choir

Offer each other a sign of God's peace.

Looking Ahead

- Prepare for your next session by prayerfully reading and studying:
    - Session 12: We Depend on God: The Lord's Prayer;
    - Scripture: Luke 11:5-13 (teachings on prayer);
    - *United States Catholic Catechism for Adults,* Chapter 36, "Jesus Taught Us to Pray," p. 487 on "Give Us This Day Our Daily Bread," p. 488 on "And Forgive Us Our Trespasses, as We Forgive Those Who Trespass against Us," pp. 488-489 on "And Lead Us Not into Temptation," and p. 489 on "But Deliver Us from Evil."
- You may like to consult the relevant paragraphs from the *Catechism of the Catholic Church:*
    - paragraphs 2828-2837 on "Give Us This Day Our Daily Bread;
    - paragraphs 2838-2845 on "And Forgive Us Our Trespasses, as We Forgive Those Who Trespass against Us";
    - paragraphs 2846-2849 on "And Lead Us Not into Temptation";
    - paragraphs 2850-2854 on "But Deliver Us from Evil."
- Remember to use RENEWING FAMILY FAITH and its helpful suggestions on how to extend the fruits of your sharing beyond your group, especially to your families. See page 93.

We Depend on God:
The Lord's Prayer

Suggested Environment

You may have a Bible—open to the reading for this session—displayed on a small table along with a burning candle. Near the Bible, you may place a loaf of bread. Consider decorating the table with the color of the liturgical season and other symbols of faith.

In addition, it is helpful to have available the Catechism of the Catholic Church (CCC) *and the* United States Catholic Catechism for Adults (USCCA).

Begin with a quiet, reflective atmosphere.

Lifting Our Hearts

Song Suggestion

"Jesus, Come to Us," David Haas

13

Prayer

Pray together.

Father,
As we come together to reflect on our faith
and on the prayer your Son has given us,
we pray that you "give us this day our daily bread,"
knowing that we depend on you for everything.

We believe that we are asking
for far more than bread,
and that all our needs
of body and spirit
will be met.

We are asking for the nourishment
of all who are hungry.

We pray that you "forgive us our trespasses,
as we forgive those who trespass against us,"
that we be forgiven to the extent that we forgive others.

We know, Lord, how impossible this is for us to do;
we know that this will be done because,
with you, "all things are possible."

Holy Spirit of discernment and strength,
"lead us not into temptation."

Amen.

Sharing Our Good News

Before continuing, take a few moments to share with the group something of your experience of prayer since our last meeting, including anything that might have resulted from "Living the Good News."

Reflection 1

We ask, God answers

Josephine Bakhita was born in Sudan in 1869 and, at the age of nine, was kidnapped by slave traders. She was so traumatized that she forgot her name and was called "Bakhita"—"fortunate one"—by her captors. She was sold several times and subjected to extreme physical and emotional cruelty, including tattooing, scarring, and severe beating, before an Italian consul bought her and took her to Italy; she was given as a gift to another family and worked for them as a nanny. When her "owners" had to move to the Black Sea region for business reasons, they left their young daughter and Josephine in the care of the Canossian Daughters of Charity in Venice. While she was with the sisters, Josephine received the sacraments. When her "owner" returned to Italy, Josephine refused to leave the sisters; Italian law was on her side, and she remained. She entered religious life in 1896 and for 50 years served with the order's community in Schio in the Province of Vicenza, cooking, sewing, embroidering, and attending to the door. During years of illness at the end of her life, she would answer inquiries about her health by saying that she was "as the Master desires."

When she was asked in later life about those who had enslaved and nearly killed her, she said, "I pity them! No doubt they were unaware of the anguish they caused me. They were the masters and I was the slave. Just as it is natural for us to do good, so it is natural for them to behave as they did behave to me. They did so out of habit, not out of wickedness." Josephine Bakhita died in 1947. She was canonized in 2000 by Pope John Paul II.

Sharing Question

• When St. Josephine Bakhita forgave those who had trespassed against her, she was forgiving people who had robbed her of her family, her youth, and her freedom, and abused her almost to the point of death. How do you forgive those whose "trespasses" have been most serious?

The final four petitions of the Lord's Prayer remind us of how much we need our Father's help and grace and how generously he responds to our needs. Jesus taught us to pray in this way because, in doing so, we acknowledge how good God is (*CCC*, 2828). These petitions also express the covenant relationship we have with our creator: "We are his and he is ours, for our sake" (*CCC*, 2829).

As we read in St. Luke's Gospel, Jesus taught us about prayers of petition, encouraging us to be trusting and, therefore, persistent in our conversation with God.

Spotlight on the *Catechism*

"The Catechism reminds us that the Lord Jesus asks us to believe in order to pray and to pray in order to believe …. Belief in the Father, Son, and Spirit should be essentially and immediately connected to a prayerful and loving communion with the Trinity.

Belief in Catholic doctrine draws us to prayer and to a divine reassurance about the validity of these revealed truths of God to which we have responded in faith. We give ourselves to prayer to deepen our personal relationship with God in a loving communion. Experiencing God in prayer shows us the vitality of the truthfulness of doctrine and puts energy into our spiritual and moral witness.

Just as the understanding of doctrine requires study and effort, so also does the practice of prayer…. Since prayer is a loving relationship with God, it places demands upon us. No love exists without sacrifice."

United States Catholic Catechism for Adults, p. 491

Pondering the Word

"Knock, and the door will be opened"

Luke 11:5-13

Sharing Questions

- Take a moment to reflect on what word, phrase, or image from the scripture passage touches your heart or speaks to your life. Reflect in silence on your thoughts, or share them aloud.

- Are you persistent in prayer, or do you easily give up? What obstacles do you encounter as you try to persevere in prayer?

> "The Our Father contains all possible petitions; we cannot conceive of any prayer not already contained in it. It is to prayer what Christ is to humanity. It is impossible to say it once through, giving the fullest possible attention to each word, without a change, infinitesimal perhaps but real, taking place in the soul."
>
> *Simone Weil*

Reflection 2

"Give us this day our daily bread"

Asking for help is not easy for those who prefer to be self-sufficient or, rather, *imagine* that they are self-sufficient. Yet throughout human history, we have learned that we are dependent on God for all our needs—including life itself. We ask for bread because we need nourishment to live, but we are really asking for more than bread. We are asking for all of our living needs. The God who created us and sustains us responds by giving us "all appropriate goods and blessings, both material and spiritual" (*CCC*, 2830). Still, we cannot ignore the fact that while God provides enough food to feed everyone on the planet, many in the world are hungry through no fault of their own (*CCC*, 2831). We Christians must confront that reality by asking God for bread to feed all people, and by cooperating with God by sharing, out of love, what he has given us (*CCC*, 2833).

As immediate as our material needs sometimes seem to be, we also ask God in this petition to feed us in a more profound way. Our need was pointedly expressed by Mother Teresa, who cited the prophecy of Amos in speaking of a famine—"not a famine of bread, nor a thirst for water, but of hearing the words of the Lord" (*Am* 8:11). We are in need of spiritual nourishment at least as urgently as we are in need of

Spotlight on the *Catechism*

"We know that preventive medicine is desirable so that curative medicine may not be needed. Preventing the possibility of sin is preferable to sinning with its negative impact on our lives. Traditionally we have been taught to avoid the occasions of sin, that is, persons or situations that may lead us to sin. Virtue grows stronger with its practice.... [We] entrust ourselves to the Holy Spirit to keep us alert to the dangers of sin and give us the grace to resist temptation."

United States Catholic Catechism for Adults, p. 488

corporal nourishment. For that reason, the *Catechism* explains, this fourth petition also concerns the sources of that nourishment: the Word of God and the Body of Christ, the Eucharist (cf. *CCC*, 2835).

"And forgive us our trespasses, as we forgive those who trespass against us"

Jesus taught this petition to his disciples, and his followers have been repeating it ever since. We Christians have recited it all our lives. Still, the *Catechism* describes it as "astonishing" (*CCC*, 2838). On the one hand, we appeal to the God who sacrificed his Son precisely so that our sins might be forgiven; on the other hand, we accept the obligation to forgive *in the same measure* those who have wronged us (*CCC*, 2838-2839). In fact, we recognize in this petition that God's mercy "cannot penetrate our hearts as long as we have not forgiven those who have trespassed against us. Love, like the Body of Christ, is indivisible; we cannot love the God we cannot see if we do not love the brother or sister we do see (Cf. 1 *Jn* 4:20) " (*CCC*, 2840). Nor does a muttered "I'm sorry" qualify as forgiveness as Jesus meant it in this prayer. He made his meaning clear in the parable of the servant whose master severely punished him for refusing to forgive the debt of a fellow slave. The parable ends with these words: "So my heavenly Father will also do to every one of you, if you do not forgive your brother or sister from your heart" (*Mt* 18:35) (*CCC*, 2843).

Sharing Our Faith

• When you ask forgiveness from God, what makes you confident in his mercy?

"And lead us not into temptation"

In this petition we ask God to help us avoid people, places, objects, thoughts, or activities that could inspire us to sin. The petition does not suggest that God would have any part in placing such things in our paths. The Greek term translated here as "lead" "means both 'do not let us enter into temptation' and 'do not let us yield to temptation' (Cf. *Mt* 6:21,24)" (*CCC*, 2846). Throughout our lives we are confronted with situations in which we must recognize good and evil and choose between them. In these situations, God gives us strength in the Holy Spirit, but we cannot succeed except through prayer. Jesus also urged us to be vigilant, to be always aware of the influences that surround us every day; in this, too, the Holy Spirit constantly seeks to keep us awake (*CCC*, 2849).

"But deliver us from evil"

We continue to pray for "us" rather than for "me" as we, together with the whole Church, ask God to deliver the human family from evil (*CCC*, 2850). In this petition, we are not referring to evil as an abstract idea but as Satan, the one who tirelessly tries to obstruct God's plan and the salvation won for us through the sacrifice and resurrection of Jesus (*CCC*, 2851). In this petition we ask God to free us from Satan and from every form of evil that he inspires (*CCC*, 2854).

"For the kingdom, the power, and the glory are yours, now and forever. Amen."

This final doxology, or praise to God, which many Christians use to close the Lord's Prayer, proclaims again our adoration and thanksgiving to God—reaffirming the first three petitions in the Lord's Prayer (*CCC*, 2855). And when we say "Amen,"—"So be it"— we confirm what we have just prayed (*CCC*, 2856)—that we believe in a God who loves us, that we praise and thank him and recognize our total dependence on him, our Father.

Sharing Questions

- Identify some conscious practices or some habits that you changed because they were keeping you or those around you from a closer relationship with God. How did that change help you?

- How has the experience of these twelve sessions helped you?

Living the Good News

Jesus emphasized the connection between faith and action, between what we believe and what we do. In that spirit, decide on an individual or group action that flows from what you have shared in this session. If you decide to act on your own, share your decision with the group. If you decide on a group action, determine among you which individual members will take responsibility for various aspects of the action.

You are likely to benefit most from taking an action that arises from your own response to the session. However, you can consider one of the following suggestions or use these ideas to help develop one of your own:

- Join a prayer group, or invite this group to continue to meet and pray together between seasons.

- Join Bread for the World, a citizen-action group seeking policy changes that will give hungry people more opportunities. Bread for the World, 50 F Street, NW, Suite 500, Washington, DC 20001. Phone: 202-639-9400. Toll free: 800-82-BREAD. Fax: 202-639-9401. Web site: www.bread.org E-mail: bread@bread.org or institute@bread.org.

- Work for legislation for a world food bank.

- Journal about those things for which you need to forgive yourself.

- Receive the sacrament of penance, and forgive those who have wronged you.

- Review reflectively the major temptations you have in your life. Pray and fast, asking God to help you overcome those temptations.

- Gather as a group to hold a special prayer and social experience to celebrate your faith, your sharing, and your Living the Good News.

- Celebrate in a special way with your group through a prayer or social event.

- Continue to meet as a small community using one of the three other books in this series: *Why Catholic? Journey through the Catechism* (see pages 92-93).

In light of this session, this week I commit to:

_____

_____

Lifting Our Hearts

Offer prayers of thanksgiving and praise to God.

Respond to each prayer: **How great and glorious is our God!**

Pray, offering each other some sign of God's peace.

To conclude, slowly pray the Lord's Prayer.

Looking Ahead

- Between Seasons of *Why Catholic?* continue meeting to faith share. Consider using the edition of PRAYERTIME: *Faith-Sharing Reflections on the Sunday Gospels*, available from RENEW International, that matches the liturgical year.

- Remember to use RENEWING FAMILY FAITH and its helpful suggestions on how to extend the fruits of your sharing beyond your group, especially to your families. See page 93.

- View and discuss Turning Points: Witness Stories, a RENEW video series at **youtube.com/user/turningpointsstories**.

- Read our inspirational reflections at **blog.renewintl.org**.

Why Catholic?
Resources from RENEW International

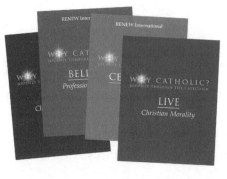

WHY CATHOLIC? Journey through the Catechism is a parish-based process of evangelization and adult faith formation from RENEW International. This process, designed for sharing in small Christian communities, is structured around exploring the important truths of our faith as they are presented in the *Catechism of the Catholic Church* and in the *United States Catholic Catechism for Adults*.

WHY CATHOLIC? helps nourish faith and enhance our sense of Catholic identity. The process and materials encourage us to understand and live the reasons why we are Catholic, and so lead us to a faith that is experienced more authentically, connecting us more deeply and meaningfully to God, and to others.

There are four books in the *WHY CATHOLIC?* series, each offering twelve sessions:

- PRAY: *Christian Prayer*
- BELIEVE: *Profession of Faith*
- CELEBRATE: *Sacraments*
- LIVE: *Christian Morality*

WHY CATHOLIC? is far more than printed resources for faith-sharing in small communities. It is a complete integrated process providing materials and support both in print and on the web, together with opportunities for faith enrichment events and retreats for the whole parish, as well as a series of training workshops for small community leaders.

For each of the four WHY CATHOLIC? books, there is a music CD. Each CD is a 12-song compilation of the songs suggested for the moments of prayer during the faith-sharing sessions. The CDs are available singly, or as a set.

Families can extend the fruits of sharing on the same themes presented in the books by using RENEWing Family Faith: attractive four-color companion bulletins with activities and reflections for sharing among different age groups.

This process of faith-building through faith-sharing is also available in Spanish: ¿POR QUÉ SER CATÓLICO?

Additional Resources

There are additional resources designed to foster the fruitful implementation of *WHY CATHOLIC?* and any faith-sharing process:

SOWING SEEDS:
Essentials for Small Community Leaders

This book offers a comprehensive collection of pastoral insights and practical suggestions to help small community leaders guide their groups in a way that nourishes spiritual growth. Culled from RENEW International's three decades of experience in pioneering and promoting small Christian communities, this book overflows with simple but effective ideas and strategies that will enhance the way these groups reflect on and respond to the Gospel.

GLEANINGS:
A Personal Prayer Journal

Many participants in small communities tell us how much they are helped in both their shared discussion and their personal reflection by the technique known as journaling: keeping a notebook for the expression of thoughts and ideas.

Gleanings is a valuable tool for both avid and occasional journal writers. Each page spread is decorated with a spiritual quotation or musing that can inspire prayerful reflection on your relationship with God. The comfortably-sized format makes it an excellent companion for your personal faith journey, helping tap into the richness of God's wisdom within you. It is also a thoughtful gift for friends or family.

PrayerTime Cycle A, B, C: Faith-Sharing Reflections on the Sunday Gospels

This faith-sharing resource responds to the U.S. Bishops' suggestion that "every parish meeting can begin with the reading of the upcoming Sunday's Gospel, followed by a time of reflection and faith sharing."

With each Sunday's Gospel as a focus, *PrayerTime* proposes meaningful reflections, focused faith-sharing questions, related questions for consideration, and prayers as a source of spiritual nourishment and inspiration.

Use *PrayerTime* any time of year, whenever the small community needs. It is also ideal for beginning meetings of the pastoral council, staff, and other parish groups. The themes can also be read personally as a way to prepare for Sunday Mass.

At Prayer with Mary

ALSO AN

eBOOK

At Prayer with Mary offers seven sessions on the life and mystery of Mary that will deepen your appreciation of and devotion to our Blessed Mother Mary and enrich your prayer experiences. Over the centuries, Mary's example has inspired Christians to imitate her by saying "yes" to God's call in their own lives. Her faithfulness, as it is portrayed in the Gospel narratives, is a model of the prayerful kind of life Jesus calls us to. Scripture, Catholic teaching, personal testimonies, and Marian prayer—including the rosary—provide a renewed appreciation of Mary's place in today's world, where she, as always, points the way to Christ.

Also available as an eBook!

This 14-song CD is also available and contains the songs suggested for use during the moments of prayer.

LONGING FOR THE HOLY:
Spirituality for Everyday Life
Based on selected insights of Ronald Rolheiser, OMI

Experience how the gentle spiritual guidance and practical wisdom of best-selling Catholic author Fr. Ronald Rolheiser, OMI can enliven everyday life. Suitable for small community faith sharing or individual reflection, *Longing for the Holy* covers different dimensions of contemporary spiritual life for those who want to enrich their sense of the presence of God and develop a deeper spirituality.

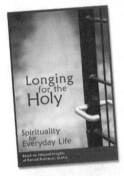

The Participant's Book contains twelve sessions with prayers, reflections, sharing questions, and stories from saints and contemporary people of faith.

This resource is also available in a four-CD set audio edition, which has both narrated text and songs for all twelve sessions.

The songs suggested for the moments of prayer in the faith-sharing sessions are offered on this 13-song anthology CD.

The kit includes the essential ingredients to bring this engaging spiritual experience to your parish or small Christian community. Purchase of the kit provides membership benefits including the opportunity for web-based workshops and faith enrichment experiences, as well as a web library of support materials.

Advent Awakenings

Advent is a time of spiritual anticipation amidst the often distracting preparations for Christmas. Stay focused on the significance of this season with *Advent Awakenings*. Each book contains four sessions corresponding with the four Sundays of Advent and presents themes drawn from the Sunday gospel readings, plus enriching devotions for family use.

Appropriate for seasonal groups, small Christian communities, and individual reflection and prayer.

This 15-song CD contains the songs suggested for use during the prayerful reflections of each faith-sharing session for years A, B, and C.

Lenten Longings
Year A, B, C

Make a six-week retreat by exploring the Sunday readings of Lent. Based on the three-year cycle of the *Lectionary*, each book contains six sessions corresponding to the six weeks of Lent and presents themes drawn from the year's Lenten readings. Simple language and everyday metaphors steep you in the season's promptings to surrender self, work for justice, and deepen prayer life. *Lenten Longings* is well suited for seasonal groups, small Christian communities, and individual reflection.

ALSO AN
BOOK

Also available as an eBook!

An 18-song CD is also available and contains the songs suggested for use during the prayerful reflections of each faith-sharing session for years A, B, and C.

Scenes from a Parish
Special Edition DVD and Film Faith Sharing Guides
In English and Spanish

Get a rare glimpse into one parish's real-world experience as it struggles to reconcile ideals of faith with the realities of today's changing and diverse culture.

View, reflect upon, and share faith with this special edition film and *Faith-Sharing Guide* and its important themes of welcoming the stranger, offering compassion, and feeding the hungry.

Ideal for parish-wide, small group, and personal viewing and reflection.

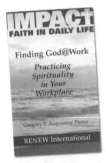

Finding God@Work

Six faith-sharing sessions guide us on a quest: can God be found at work? If so, how? Examine your lived experience of work—both positively and negatively—from a spiritual vantage point, considering relevant passages from Scripture, and principles of Catholic social teaching.

Forgiveness and Reconciliation

The insightful wisdom and many inspiring stories of forgiveness and reconciliation offer a profound understanding of people's desire to be forgiven and the steps to take to live reconciled lives. Reflect on the healing power of God and the richness of the sacrament of reconciliation to discover again how to live in the freedom of God.

For more information or to order these and other fine resources from RENEW International, please visit our secure online bookstore at www.renewintl.org/store or use our toll free order line: 1-888-433-3221.

Did you know...?

**RENEW
INTERNATIONAL**

RENEW International is a not-for-profit Catholic ministry organization that has touched the lives of 25 million people in the United States, Canada, and 22 other countries.

From the inner city and rural areas to remote parts of the developing world, RENEW International's priority is to serve all parishes who desire to renew their faith and build the Church, regardless of their economic situation.

Throughout RENEW's dynamic history, individuals have generously reached out to support our mission.

Please join us by making a donation to RENEW International at **www.renewintl.org/donate**

Interested in learning more about RENEW?

World RENEW, our free eNewsletter, covers interesting topics on today's spiritual life with behind-the-scenes stories and special features on RENEW International's work with parishes and small communities around the world.

To read more and explore how you can be an integral part of the RENEW International family, please visit **www.renewintl.org/subscribe**

Connect with us!

 facebook.com/RENEWIntl

BLOG **blog.renewintl.org**

@RENEWIntl

You Tube **youtube.com/RENEWInternational**

Notes